IT'S NOT YOU

27 (WRONG) REASONS
YOU'RE SINGLE

SARA ECKEL

A PERIGEE BOOK

A PERIGEE BOOK
Published by the Penguin Group
Penguin Group (USA) LLC
375 Hudson Street, New York, New York 10014

USA • Canada • UK • Ireland • Australia • New Zealand • India • South Africa • China

penguin.com

A Penguin Random House Company

Library of Congress Cataloging-in-Publication Data

Eckel, Sara.
It's not you : 27 (wrong) reasons you're single / Sara Eckel.— First edition.
pages cm
ISBN 978-0-399-16287-9 (pbk.)
1. Single people. 2. Single women. 3. Man-woman relationships.
4. Interpersonal relations. I. Title.
HQ800.E254 2014
302—dc23 2013032620

First edition: January 2014

PRINTED IN THE UNITED STATES OF AMERICA

10 9 8 7 6 5 4 3 2 1

Text design by Laura K. Corless

Portions of this book appeared in a different form in the *New York Times* and *Self* magazine.
For the subjects' privacy, some names and identifying details have been changed.

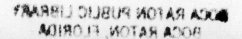

"*It's Not You* masquerades as self-help, but it's really a manifesto, a radical declaration of truths that shouldn't be all that radical but somehow are nonetheless. Sara Eckel does what no one writing about singleness has yet had the guts to do. She points out that coupling up is often nothing more than a matter of luck and that conventional wisdom about love is no substitute for real wisdom about life—something she has in spades."
　　　　　　　　　　　　　　—Meghan Daum, author of *My Misspent Youth*

"Finally! Someone said it: Being single does not mean you're broken. Thank you, Sara Eckel, for speaking up and turning the tables on anyone who dared point their needling finger at poor old singletons negotiating the process of looking for love. *It's Not You* is a smart and sane respite from the incessant chatter of relationship self-help that places the single person in the middle of a perpetual makeover project. Eckel deftly argues why you don't need any of it, and she'll make you think about dating in an entirely new light. Her book is fresh, relatable, funny, and empowering, and I'm only one percent mad at her for not writing it sooner. Mostly, I just want to hug her, and so will you."
　　　　　　　　　　　　　　—Rachel Machacek, author of *The Science of Single*

"Debunking the myths and well-meaning advice lobbed onto single women today, Sara Eckel's *It's Not You* is like soothing guidance from a best friend in book form. Fearless, funny, and wise, it's a reminder to single women everywhere that the best antidote to the overwhelmingly negative dating feedback that prevails is self-compassion."
　　　　　　　　　　　　　　—Ava Chin, "Urban Forager" columnist and author of *Eating Wildly*

continued . . .

"Sara Eckel has composed an electrically charged response to a world still eager to tie a woman's value to her marital status. *It's Not You* is a thorough and thoughtful debunking of the myths of blame routinely foisted on women who have not (yet or ever) found mates. Eckel is funny, compassionate, and righteously resistant to the lies women are told about how personal shortcomings have damned them to singlehood, while smartly standing up to assumptions that there's anything wrong with unmarried life to begin with."

—Rebecca Traister, author of *Big Girls Don't Cry*

"*It's Not You* is a funny, thoughtful, and long-overdue response to every well-intentioned tool who insists single women are single because they're 'too' something: picky, available, desperate, intimidating, nice, negative, attractive, or, I don't know, averse to clog dancing. Instead, she assures us we're fine. The only problem? We simply haven't met the guy of our dreams yet."

—Diane Mapes, author of *How to Date in a Post-Dating World*

"Sara Eckel counters prevailing myths about dating and marriage, and offers solace and very helpful advice to those who feel pained by prolonged singlehood. Above all, this book will resonate with readers because of the way she shares her own struggling, vulnerable heart."

—Gabriel Cohen, author of *Storms Can't Hurt the Sky*

"Part Buddhist teacher and part social critic, Sara Eckel tells single women what we older-to-marry folks wish we could go back to say to our own younger self-doubting unmarried selves. . . . This book is a refreshing study of women realizing the best potential of feminism: to realistically accept both the challenges, and the triumphs, of living life on one's own terms."

—Paula Kamen, author of *Her Way, All in My Head*, and *Finding Iris Chang*

CONTENTS

CONTENTS

WHAT'S WRONG WITH YOU?

We met in a bar in Brooklyn, a hipster version of an old Italian social club. He was nice-enough-looking, a bit grayer and heavier than his profile picture, but no doubt so was I. We chatted about the neighborhood—the dog park we liked, the Asian fusion restaurant we were sorry was closing—and gave each other vital stats—years lived in New York, number of brothers and sisters.

"How long has it been since your last relationship?" he asked, his voice clipped, a dental hygienist inquiring about my flossing routine.

"Three years," I lied. The truth was closer to six.

He leaned back, looking at me in a cool and curious way,

like I was a restaurant with too few customers, a house that had been listed too long.

"What's wrong with you?" he asked.

"I don't know," I said.

"But you're attractive?" he asked, as if he wasn't sure anymore. As if I could help him out with this.

"I don't know what to tell you," I said. "I don't know why."

Of course, I was outraged. I finished my ginger old-fashioned. I said I had to get up early. But in truth, his question was no worse than the one I asked myself nearly every day. It wasn't full-blown self-loathing, more a feeling that snuck up unawares, a hollowness that hit me in the chest at certain times—a long subway ride home from a mediocre date, a Sunday-night phone conversation with a married friend who suddenly says she has to go, her husband just took the roast out of the oven.

Why was I unable to find the thing that mattered to me most? I was trying so hard—obeying the incessant drumbeat to "get out there," dutifully mining my psyche for any emotional blockages that might be preventing me from finding lifelong love. I took hour-long commutes to attend the birthday parties of coworkers' friends and went to the midnight shows of college acquaintances' bands. I spent countless hours and dollars on yoga, gym memberships, and other forms of personal maintenance. And yet, there it was. I was a woman in her late thirties, alone. What was wrong? What was wrong with *me*?

As I speak with other people who stayed single well into their adulthood—and whose unattached state was not a choice—I hear that toxic question more than any other. These are intelligent, grown-up professionals—newspaper reporters, university professors, entrepreneurs—who drive their mothers to the doctor and look after their nieces and nephews. They have close friends, solid workout routines, and positions on their local community boards.

But that one thing is missing, and many singles can't pretend it doesn't matter to them.

As much as they would like to live up to the cultural ideal of the perfectly autonomous singleton—that fiery free spirit who won't be weighed down by a relationship—that's not their reality. They don't want to settle, but they do want a partner. And so they ask the question—why? In this earnest soul-search, they find many different, often conflicting explanations:

"You're too picky."

"You're too desperate."

"You're too independent."

"You're too needy."

"You're too intimidating."

"You're too negative."

"You're too unrealistic."

"You have low self-esteem."

When you're a single person who would rather not be, the pathologies are endless. Even when you push back—"What do you mean I'm too independent? Are you suggesting I quit my job and move in with my parents?"—the sheer number of possible explanations can make even the most self-possessed singleton doubt herself. Surely *one* of them must stick.

We're a nation that believes strongly in personal efficacy—if there's something in your life that isn't working quite the way you'd like, then the problem must begin and end with you. Even people diagnosed with serious illnesses are instructed to maintain a positive attitude, as if *that* will make the cancer go away. Many of these prescriptions come from a well-intentioned place—of course, it *is* a good idea to take charge of your life and work toward a happier future. Of course, we understand that if we crave life's rewards—interesting jobs, nice homes, rich social networks—we'll need to apply ourselves.

But the myth that we're 100 percent in control of what happens in our lives makes us extremely hard on ourselves, and single people especially, so eager to solve this riddle of Why, are often willing to accept the premise that some fatal personality flaw is preventing them from finding lifelong love.

For me, solace came from the place where single women usually take comfort: my other single friends. We'd gather on Friday and Saturday nights, swapping funny and tragic stories of our dismal dating lives, reassuring one another of our collective beauty, intelligence, and kindness, marveling at the idiocy of men who failed to see this in our friends.

Mostly, we would try to make sense of it all. Why wasn't this happening? Were our married friends really so much more desirable or emotionally healthy than we were? Once in a while, someone would declare that married women were actually quite miserable, that *they* envied *us*. But this theory never got too far— we knew our married friends wouldn't switch places with us, no matter how much they complained about their husbands.

Of course, there are many popular books and television shows that detail the lives of such women, but in those stories adorable, self-deprecating men constantly approach the heroines in parks and bus stops and ask them to dinner. Even in her edgier iterations, the sitcom single woman never stays alone for long. Instead, she skips from one sexy-but-flawed man to the next. My friends and I had various dates and mini-relationships, but mostly we were alone.

We had each other of course, but not in the perfectly synced way our television counterparts did. We didn't live in the same apartment building and pop in unannounced to make grilled-cheese sandwiches or coach each other for job interviews. We weren't always available for emergency brunches or last-minute trips to Jamaica. Instead, we had complicated, independent lives wending down many different paths, lives that sometimes had us working sixteen-hour days, or moving out of state, or navigating a fledging romance. We saw each other the way most urban professionals do—by booking dates days or weeks in advance. That meant that we were frequently alone, with time.

Since I believed the conventional wisdom that I could "work on myself" in order to be "ready for love," I approached those quiet evenings and weekends with industry. I knew the deal: If I was looking for another person to make me happy, I'd be sorely disappointed. No one would love me until I learned to love myself. So: Time to get crackin'!

In many ways, I did "improve." I conquered my fear of public speaking, taught myself to cook, learned to do a handstand. I also expanded my social circle—throwing dinner parties, joining summer-house shares, attending artist colonies. I had a lot of fun and made many new friends. But I was still unattached, and in the dark of Saturday night, I still wondered: "What's wrong with me?"

On my first date with Mark, he asked the dreaded question: "How long has it been?" I looked at the table and cupped my hand around my beer. The answer—eight years—was not one I cared to share.

It shouldn't have mattered. Mark and I had worked together for two months. He had been hanging around my office, sending flirty emails, and—most adorable to me, and horrifying to him—blushing whenever we spoke. He was kind of in the bag.

But I still didn't want to answer.

"A long time," I said instead, rolling my eyes, hoping he was one of those people who thought six months was "long."

I came clean a few weeks later, after we'd snuck out of the office to drink coffee and kiss. "There's something I have to tell you," I said gravely, as if preparing to reveal a fatal disease or a husband in New Jersey. I took a deep breath and told him I hadn't had a boyfriend for nearly a decade, and not for lack of trying.

Mark shrugged. "Lucky for me. All those other guys were idiots."

And that was it. To Mark, I wasn't a problem to solve, a puzzle that needed working out. I was a girl he was falling in love with, just as I was falling in love with him. Mark wasn't looking for the cultural ideal of a marriageable female— whatever that means. He just wanted me.

Less than a year later, Mark and I were living together. Four years after that, we married. My friends came to our wedding in a small Brooklyn park—and some brought their husbands.

I have friends who are still looking, friends who are married, and friends who are divorced. The difference, I've come to see, is largely due to chance, rather than character. Because after all those years of self-doubt, my late-marrying friends and I found men who love us even though we're still cranky and neurotic, even though we still haven't got our careers together, even though we sometimes talk too loud or drink too much or swear at the TV when the news is on. We have gray hairs and unfashionable clothes and bad attitudes. They love us, anyway.

What's wrong with me? What's wrong with any of us? If we're honest, the answer probably is "plenty." But that's not the point.

Who Do You Think You Are?

When Tibetan Buddhist scholar Chögyam Trungpa first came to the West to study psychology at Oxford in the 1960s, he was surprised to discover the concept of "original sin" was not only a religious belief but also a foundation of secular psychological thought. "Among patients, theoreticians, and therapists alike, there seems to be great concern with the idea of some original mistake, which causes later suffering—a kind of punishment for that mistake," he wrote in *The Sanity We Are Born With*. "One finds that a sense of guilt or being wounded is quite pervasive. Whether or not such people actually believe in the idea of original sin, or in God for that matter, they seem to feel that they have done something wrong in the past and are now being punished for it."

Tibetan Buddhism, he explained, takes a different view—everything is basically good. One useful image is a golden statue buried in mud. Rather than possessing some deeply rooted flaw that must be eradicated, we merely need to hose down all the muck and shit that we lay on ourselves—*I'm too this, I'm not enough that*. When we peel off those dark layers, we're left with a simple being that needs no improvement.

That central idea is radically different from our culture's, where alternating voices of cheerleading and shame continually urge us to better ourselves. I'm not saying that's always wrong, but I think it's worth examining, especially for those caught in the "What's wrong with me?" trap. To that end, I've structured this book around the messages that singles, especially single women, get about who they are and who they're supposed to be. They come from self-help books, cultural commentaries, trend stories, matchmaking programs, Internet dates, and beloved friends and family who want the best for us but often don't have a clue.

The purpose isn't to lampoon dating gurus—who, let's face it, can be pretty slow-moving targets—or gin up grudges against the people who care about you, but to help unwind all that crazy-making feedback in the hope that it might help you uncover your own instincts.

Before we begin, some caveats:

I'm not an expert—I don't have a PhD or a reality show. I'm

a freelance writer who has reported stories on emotional well-being for many years and a beginning student of Tibetan Buddhism.

I don't presume to speak for all singles. Of course, many people are happily unattached or are searching but don't trouble themselves with the question "What's wrong?"

I have a very particular point of view—straight, white, childless, middle-class woman. I'm aware that this perspective is far from universal—that not everything in this book will necessarily apply to men, single parents, gays and lesbians, and those who grew up in households that did not resemble a 1950s sitcom quite as much as mine did. Despite these limitations, I believe there is a common experience that many longtime singles have—one that transcends gender, race, or sexual orientation—and I hope this book will be useful to anyone struggling with these issues.

The people I've interviewed for this book, both those directly quoted and those whose experiences have informed it in a more general way, are for the most part women who, like me, were single for a significant part of their adult life—some now married, others not. I use the word "marriage" loosely—I'm talking about committed monogamous partnerships, regardless of whether the parties are legally entitled to each other's Social Security or health insurance benefits.

Finally, I've focused on women because we're the ones who

get the most instruction on who we're supposed to be—and, let's face it—we're the ones who more often take it.

That said, after I published what I thought was my very particular story in the *New York Times* "Modern Love" column, I discovered that my experience was far more widespread than I could have imagined.

"I am a twenty-five-year-old boy who lives in Sao Paulo, Brazil. Last night I went to bed thinking exactly what you mentioned in your article: 'What is wrong with me?'"

"I am a journalist from India though I am currently working and living in Dubai, UAE. . . . A friend in the U.S. forwarded this piece to me a few weeks ago when I was going through a very low phase. And I have been reading it, rereading it and re-rereading it, and posting it to my single and married girlfriends, all of whom have the same reaction as I did—this is so me."

"[Your article] instantly echoed with me and my single friends, resulting in so many of them reposting the article right after reading it on social websites, in China actually."

Closer to home, a thirty-three-year-old investment banker wrote to tell me she bookmarked the essay on her browser and rereads it about once a week. A twenty-four-year-old Harvard Medical School student said the piece brought her calm in the midst of a flurry of wedding invitations. A seventy-one-year-old woman reported that she married for the first time the previous summer. "Thank goodness I lived long enough!" she said.

Single women told me they printed the essay and carried it with them in their purses to reread when they were feeling down. Single men told me they struggled with the same issues, albeit without a cadre of supportive same-sex friends to commiserate with (actually, many single women said that too). Married women who, like me, found their soul mate after spending many years on their own shared their own, very similar experiences. After years and even decades of self-questioning, they at last stumbled upon the guy who *liked* their short hair, their dark humor, their twenty extra pounds. "All the things that I thought a man would hate about me (hello, two cats), he adores. All my quirks that I thought I'd have to apologize for, he gets," wrote a forty-two-year-old woman who had married the year before.

What was most striking about the letters was their similarity. Despite the many different ages and backgrounds, hundreds of readers said essentially the same thing—*You are me. Your story is mine.*

For a writer, there's nothing more gratifying than discovering that you have accessed a direct connection to so many varied souls. But I think the reason my story resonated was not because I told people something they didn't know, but because I told them something they *did* know. I think I reminded them of their innate worthiness, so deeply mired under the mud of advice and cultural commentary. I think I reconnected them with a small kernel of wisdom they already had, one that said, *I don't think I need to change. I think I'm perfectly lovable, exactly as I am.*

This book is not a guide for how to find a husband or wife—because I have no idea. It's also not an action plan for renovating your soul so that you'll be "ready" for love; if you've picked up this book, I'm sure you're plenty ready. It's not a tome from a know-it-all married lady—because seriously, I just met a dude, that's it.

Instead, it's my attempt to clear away some of the societal muck that weighs us down and alienates us from our own instincts. This, of course, is not just a single-person problem—it's an everybody problem. But when you're single, there is so very much shit to wade through.

When you stop picking apart your personality and endlessly replaying the game tapes of your previous relationships, you clear a lot of mental space. When you stop letting external voices freak you out—"Better snap that guy up!" "You're not getting any younger!" "Just who do you think you are?"—you can start to tap into your own wisdom about who and what is right for you.

1

YOU HAVE ISSUES

When I was thirty-one, I quit my job and broke up with my boyfriend in the same month.

The timing was mostly coincidental—the resignation the result of a slow, methodical transition to full-time freelance writing, the breakup a rash decision based on a crush. In the span of a few weeks, I had decimated my life. All that was left was a freaked-out woman in a three-hundred-square-foot studio with a small desk, a rickety futon, and a heart full of unrequited longing. I'd wake most nights at the usual witching hours—three, four—sitting up straight on the futon, staring out my one window, wondering what the fuck I had just done.

But I had no regrets. Yes, I had blown my life to smithereens, but I would rebuild! I would take this cold cement foundation and create, brick by brick, the life I wanted, become the person I wanted to be—namely, a woman who the men I loved would love back.

Thus began the construction of Sara 2.0, a task that dovetailed neatly with my new career, writing about relationships and personal growth for magazines. Over the next several years, I interviewed psychology professors and therapists, shamelessly peppering the conversation with anecdotes from my own life— the nonstarter relationships, the failed dates, the witty, handsome men who steadfastly refused to love me.

I also talked to many self-help authors, each with a fix-it plan tailored to their persona. There was the Tough-Love Married Lady, who declared the key to finding a soul mate was to quit whining, get real, and for goodness' sake put on a little lipstick. There was the Magical Soul-Mate Finder, who prescribed journaling, nature hikes, candlelit bubble baths, and other hocuspocus. There was the Man—i.e., a moderately cute guy who wrote a book—who gave insider tips on how to hook up with him, which usually involved not being critical and having long hair.

So I grew my hair out. I took bubble baths. But mostly, I started examining my issues. Was my failure a result of my latent commitment phobia (cleverly masked as really wanting commitment), as one helmet-haired expert implied? Did I feel inherently unworthy and broadcast that low self-assessment to every man I met? (Another gentle suggestion.) Did my failure to "love myself" mean I was unable to love another?

The author who posited the commitment-phobia theory was a brassy shrink with a Dr.-First-Name moniker and a cache of rhyming, trademark-protected aphorisms. In a mildly scolding voice, she explained that if I thought a particular guy stopped calling me because he was afraid of commitment, then I had to ask myself if it was *me* who feared commitment.

I remember sitting at my desk, phone cradled under my chin, thinking, okay, this woman is cheesy and annoying, but *she makes good sense.*

Because when I looked back on all the men I'd dated, they fell into two distinct categories—those I had broken up with, and those who broke up with me. The guys I ended things with arguably would have continued to see me had I not been so terrified of committing. I dealt with this fear by preferring the guys who broke up with *me* (or who were never interested in the first place), aka the commitment-phobes. I must have wanted the commitment-phobes because *I* was a commitment-phobe.

Thus I skated in these perfect circles of logic; ignoring the many areas of my life where I had no problem committing—leases, work assignments, dinner plans (this last point might not win me any humanitarian awards, but in New York City it's a notable trait)—and brushing aside the hard-core fact that many of the men who lost (or never had) interest in me proceeded to commit to other women.

I was just relieved to have an explanation—that meant there was something to "work on," something to *do*. I could confront my commitment issues—try to be more reliable, get a dog.

But even if I had dispensed with this explanation, of course there were many others to explore. Maybe was I too needy, or too independent? Too desperate, or too picky? Too close to my father, or not close enough?

I pored over the data, creating an extremely detailed roster of my flaws and inadequacies, and emerged with a portrait of a self-conscious, frequently anxious insomniac who likes her wine a little too much and is capable of morphing into a snake-haired harpy when arguing about health care or gun control.

A lot to work on.

And work I did: To develop confidence, I took acting lessons. To expand my soul, I taught writing to disadvantaged kids. I also bought an apartment, adopted a sweet rescue dog named Taffy (commitment!), and became a regular at my local yoga center. I went down the checklist of all the things that could possibly be "wrong" and found a rich, fulfilling counterweight. When I went to parties or met men on Internet dates, I walked into the room with a straight spine and a confident smile. *See how together I am? See how happy? See how perfectly autonomous as a single person—yet also radiating the necessary warmth and vulnerability to let you in?*

I had a lot of fun, made many friends, traveled to foreign countries—the whole happy-single-woman shebang. But my love life, when it existed at all, was a random assortment of tepid dates, weird make-out sessions, and two-month what-the-hell-was-thats.

Meanwhile, people all around me fell in love like there was nothing to it. They moved in together, got married, had babies—often without the benefit of a single yoga class! I didn't get it. *I* was the one reading all the books. *I* was the one confronting my issues.

My frustration came to a head while visiting a friend in Oregon. At the time she was living in a 1920s lake-house bungalow with her cute, friendly musician boyfriend. I was bitterly envious. But more than that, I was confused—why was it never me? I spent the week venting, complaining about how unfair life was, wondering aloud what was wrong with me. My friend, quite naturally, became annoyed.

"You're not going to find anyone until you get right with yourself," she said.

I lost it—what did she think I'd been doing all this time? And anyway, what was up with this idea that self-actualization was a prerequisite to a relationship? I knew plenty of happily married people who lugged around suitcases full of hang-ups. If everyone had to "get right with themselves" before finding a partner, the population would have died off long ago.

These points, I would later learn, are supported by clinical research. University of Washington psychologist John Gottman—a marriage researcher famous for his 91 percent accuracy in predicting which newlywed couples will ultimately divorce—found that everyday neuroses do *not* hinder success in marriage.

"You might assume that people with hang-ups would be ill-suited to marriage," he and coauthor Nan Silver wrote in *The Seven Principles for Making Marriage Work.* "But research has found only the weakest connection between run-of-the-mill neuroses and falling in love. The reason: We all have our crazy buttons—issues we're not totally rational about. But they don't interfere with marriage. The key to a happy marriage isn't having a 'normal' personality but finding someone with whom you mesh."

It turns out you can be happily married even if you never resolve your issues with your mother or your weight—a fact that becomes completely intuitive when you think of any three married people you know.

Sure, there are those whose emotional problems—from garden-variety intimacy fears to full-blown personality disorders—prevent them from being in committed relationships. The problem is, these pat conclusions have been lobbed at *all* singles seeking love. Unless you declare that your unattached state is completely chosen (which will arouse suspicions of another kind) the odor of "what's the deal?" will hang in the air.

What if your only "issue" is the belief that you have them and that they're keeping you from a relationship? What if you stopped defining yourself as someone who is afraid of intimacy or attracted to the wrong kind of man? What if you instead saw yourself as a flawed but basically lovable human being? What if the only reason you're alone is you just haven't met your partner yet?

2

YOU HAVE
LOW SELF-ESTEEM

After being unattached for nine years, my friend Marcella was convinced that she had some serious deficiencies. She spent countless hours sifting through them on her therapist's couch. An artist and entrepreneur, Marcella was open to the idea that her deep interest in her work and complete apathy toward fashion or beauty treatments could be part of the problem. She gamely took her shrink's suggestion to hire a makeup artist and a personal shopper, as well as a friend's advice to smile constantly. "I said, 'Okay, I'm going to go out and smile all the time.' Well, that lasted about four minutes," Marcella said.

And, of course, she worked on her self-esteem. "But it's hard to feel really good about yourself when the guy you really enjoyed talking to never called you again. You thought you had this really energetic vibe and then . . . nothing. You keep trying to makes sense of it and you conclude it must be all me, there's all this stuff wrong with me," she said. Marcella informed me that she has tiny broken blood vessels on her face—I had known her for years and never noticed them. "At one point I thought, I'm never going to get married because of these little broken blood vessels. You start to examine everything," she said.

To the casual observer, Marcella could look like a textbook case of the neurotic single woman, smiling insanely and fretting about her blood vessels, or the career-obsessed frump, studying Klee and Kandinsky when she should have been learning how to tie a scarf or apply eye shadow. And she often felt that way. But despite all this, Marcella did in fact meet a nice man on a biking trip when she was thirty-eight, and they married and had a daughter several years later.

But it has been an uphill climb, right? Surely all those negative feelings about herself have made it tough for Marcella to love someone else? Well, no. Marcella reports that both she and her husband have self-esteem that veers toward the low side, but they think the world of each other.

You can't love another until you love yourself. This is what we tell single people, usually after some devastating blow—the

9

guy you went on five wonderful dates with stops calling, or you find yourself alone on New Year's Eve, just like last year. You feel miserable, lonely, like a bizarre outlier in a world full of happy (or happy-ish, anyway) couples.

So you pick up a women's magazine or flip on a ladies' chat show or call a friend, and you see that recurring diagnosis: low self-esteem. For singles especially, this is the grandmama of all maladies, the origin of everything from excessive pickiness to outright desperation.

We're told to love ourselves, believe in ourselves, feel good about ourselves. The only problem: How are you supposed to have high self-esteem when you feel like shit?

The answers range from cringe-inducing—stand in front of a mirror and recite phony affirmations about how wonderful you are—to things that are probably a good idea anyway, like volunteering at a food pantry. Except the point isn't to help the poor. The point is to think highly of yourself—sort of like doing community service to impress the law-school admissions officer. Only this time the gatekeeper is you, and the sales pitch—the one about how soulful and giving you are—is delivered to the harshest of critics.

But hey, whatever works, right? The more we like ourselves, the more others will like us, right?

Actually, no. Research shows that people with high self-esteem are no more well-liked than those with low self-esteem—

they only *think* they are more admired, says Kristin Neff, a psychology professor at the University of Texas at Austin. One study of college students with high self-esteem found some very informed detractors—their roommates, who weren't nearly as impressed with the self-loving subjects as they were with themselves.

But the bigger problem with self-esteem is that it's contingent on success. So it doesn't work when you need it most—like after the guy from (what you thought was) a great date blows you off. In her book, *Self-Compassion*, Neff explains that when people who have high self-esteem don't receive good reviews they feel just as bad about themselves as people with low self-esteem. When people with high self-esteem mess up—say by forgetting their lines in a play or losing the softball game for the team—they're just as likely as the low self-esteemers to think "I'm such a loser!" or "I wish I could die!"

"High self-esteem tends to come up empty-handed when the chips are down," she wrote.

But here's the good news: There are people who weather life's indignities without much damage to their self-worth. When they experience failure, embarrassment, or less-than-glowing feedback, they don't cover their eyes and mutter, "Stupid, stupid, stupid." Instead, they tell themselves things like, "Everybody goofs up now and then," or, "In the grand scheme of things, this really doesn't matter."

These are people with self-compassion, a concept that has recently attracted a great deal of study by Neff and others. People with self-compassion don't try to convince themselves and others of their greatness; they simply focus on treating themselves kindly. "These are two very different things," Neff told me.

When you're single, there is an understandable compulsion to present the shiny, high-self-esteem version of yourself. It's what, we're told, is attractive to the opposite sex. It can also help you maintain your dignity in a world that can be quite condescending toward singles. The trouble is, in our understandable efforts to prevent anyone from pitying us, we often end up being very hard on ourselves.

You feel funky because you're the only single person at the dinner party, but instead of recognizing the emotional challenge of the situation, you criticize yourself for not rising above it. Your assistant tells you she's engaged, and you cringe at the insincerity in your voice when you say "I'm so happy for you!" You spend twenty minutes wondering why he didn't call, and then berate yourself for being such a chick-flick cliché.

Most of us are much meaner to ourselves than we are to our friends—or even our enemies—which is why Neff advises talking to yourself as you would a good friend: "I'm so sorry you're in a bad place today, but these feelings you're having sound pretty normal to me. So why don't you ease up on yourself? We all feel weak or insecure sometimes. You're not alone."

This type of self-talk can shift the energy, not only making you kinder to yourself, but also to others. For example, consider that perennial self-esteem underminer: the guy who says he's going to call, but doesn't. After several days, you shoot him a quick text, some breezy observation regarding a shared joke. His response: "LOL!" And that's it.

So you get it. He's just not that into you. Et cetera. You understand there's no choice but to move on, but it still hurts—a lot. At this point, there are many ways to relate to yourself. You could torture yourself with the question "Why?" Were you not pretty enough? Smart enough? Was he put off because you mentioned you liked that cheesy sitcom or confessed that you don't have a good relationship with your sister? Asking why feels productive—you're learning from your mistakes!—but it's just another way of beating yourself up. (Especially since in my experience those questions quickly morph into statements. "I wasn't pretty enough. I wasn't smart enough. . . .")

You could also beat *him* up—a popular strategy with the self-esteemed. What kind of jerk doesn't want to be with someone as amazing as you? Clearly, he's intimidated by strong women. He probably couldn't handle the fact that you own a house or know the executive chef. Or maybe he's a serial dater, a professional cad deft at manipulating women's feelings. Whoever he is, this guy has *serious problems.*

Finally, there's the self-compassion approach. Instead of assigning blame, you simply take a moment and acknowledge the painful disappointment you're feeling. You don't try to talk yourself out of feeling bad—since feeling bad is a completely natural response to rejection. Instead, you channel that good friend: "Wow, I'm so sorry you're going through this. I know it must be hard and confusing. I wish there was more I could do to make you feel better, but you know this feeling will pass. We all get rejected sometimes. No matter what happened with this guy, you deserve a great relationship."

With self-compassion, you don't need to bolster yourself up tear anyone else down. You don't have to waste energy on the pep talk because you already know you're just fine, regardless of what this or that dude thinks.

Not only does self-compassion soften life's blows, it can also strengthen your ability to bounce back. Neff explains that although we think being critical of ourselves will spur us into action, actually, the opposite is true. Think about it: You could spend the days or weeks after getting jilted contemplating all the possible reasons why that guy didn't think you were girlfriend material—how he thought your musical tastes were pedestrian or was embarrassed that you couldn't throw a Frisbee. Or you could decide to be extra nice to yourself—get an unlimited yoga card, take your lunch in the park, see a Bette Davis double feature. Which will make you more likely to date again?

3

YOU'RE TOO NEGATIVE

Concerned about global warming? Appalled by the way money corrupts the democratic process? Notice that the restaurant manager is bullying his staff? If you're on a date, better keep those observations to yourself.

Experts might disagree on how assertive or vulnerable or chatty one should be with the opposite sex, but on the subject of optimism we see near universal consensus: Smile, sweetheart.

And who could argue with that? We all know people who whine and complain endlessly, or whose depression puts them in a state of near paralysis. So obviously certain conversation topics—your meth-addicted father, your knee surgery—usually make lousy getting-to-know-you conversation fodder.

But most of us already have the social grace to not overshare about our tax audits or plantar warts. Unfortunately, the incessant mantra of "be positive" implies that anyone who doesn't like her job or has a complicated relationship with her family—a fairly wide swath of the population—must paper over these edgy truths with perky platitudes about bosses who are tough but fair.

Even though I've always had what I consider a . . . realistic view of life, I tried to obey the common wisdom and keep it light and upbeat when dating.

Sometimes the tone would stay that way, and we'd have a pleasant enough evening, talking about the work we enjoyed and vacations we were looking forward to. But those dates are mostly forgotten. The really good dates were the ones where we shed the positivity facade fairly quickly. The ones where we talked about divorce and stepfamilies and melting ice caps. The ones where we forgot to censor ourselves, forgot to *sell* ourselves and just *were* ourselves—two somewhat lonely human beings trying to figure it all out. (One of the things I liked about Internet dating was that it brings everyone to ground level—when you meet online with a Saturday-at-ten-p.m. time stamp, you can't play the my-life-is-amazing card.)

Obviously, I'm not everyone's dream date. Sure, *some* people would prefer that, when asked about your loathsome job, you take the advice of one pop psychologist: "Well, I don't know if

I can say the *work* is fun, but the people are great!" Some people hate the sound of bad news.

On the other hand, some of us hate the sound of bullshit. Some of us would rather hear, "You know, I've been doing this for fifteen years and I really don't like the direction my profession is headed in, and I'm honestly pretty confused about what to do next." Whether a person is a "downer" or refreshingly honest is a matter of taste.

Still, even if the dating gurus go overboard, wouldn't cultivating a positive attitude be a, you know, positive thing to do?

Not necessarily. In *The Antidote: Happiness for People Who Can't Stand Positive Thinking,* journalist Oliver Burkeman explains how trying to suppress negative thoughts can actually make them *more* prevalent, a phenomena called "ironic process theory."

Most of us have done the thought experiment where you're instructed not to think of pink elephants, and then of course discover that trying to banish anything from your mind makes it more prevalent—trying *not* to think of pink elephants wildly ratchets up your awareness of pink elephants. This is why instructions to "think positively" don't work. "A person who has resolved to 'think positive' must constantly scan his or her mind for negative thoughts—there's no other way the mind could ever gauge its success at the operation—yet that scanning will draw attention to the presence of negative thoughts," wrote Burkeman.

In one experiment, people who were told not to feel sad about an unfortunate event were more distressed than those who received no instruction. Another study found that anxiety sufferers who listened to relaxation tapes had faster heart rates than those who listened to audiobooks on non-relaxation-related topics. After the death of a loved one, people who suppress their grief take longer to heal than those who allow themselves to feel the pain of their loss. And it turns out, positive affirmations aren't just embarrassing—one study found that people with low self-esteem actually felt *worse* after reciting the affirmation "I am a lovable person."

"From this perspective, the relentless cheer of positive thinking begins to seem less like an expression of joy and more like a stressful effort to stamp out any trace of negativity. . . . A positive thinker can never relax, lest an awareness of sadness or failure creep in," wrote Burkeman in the *New York Times*.

The "be positive" advice makes you fear the dark. You've got all the lights turned on, constantly vigilant. Rather than trying to eradicate negativity, Burkeman takes inspiration from the Buddhists: It's a far more effective strategy to clearly see unfortunate circumstances or unpleasant emotions for what they are—part of life, nothing to freak out about. He sums up this philosophy with words from 1960s counterculture philosopher Alan Watts: "When you try to stay on the surface of the water, you sink. But when you try to sink, you float."

This is the best dating advice I've ever heard. Instead of suppressing whatever cocktail of feelings—anxiety, ambivalence, lust—that's brewing as you walk into that restaurant, why not just note them and barrel on ahead?

Dating is an act of outrageous vulnerability. You're leaving the comfort of your home and your friends to subject yourself to the scrutiny of strangers. You're sliding into that restaurant booth, plopping your laptop and gym bag on the floor, and saying, "Hi, I'm Sara. Let's see if we can start a life together, shall we?"

It doesn't get more optimistic than that.

4

YOU'RE TOO LIBERATED

In 1970, an Australian university student scribbled *A woman needs a man like a fish needs a bicycle* on two bathroom walls—one at a bar, the other at her university. She was paraphrasing a line from one of her philosophy texts—"a man needs God like a fish needs a bicycle"—and having a bit of fun. "My inspiration arose from being involved in the renascent women's movement at the time, and from being a bit of a smart-arse," wrote Irina Dunn, who later became a member of the Australian Senate.

Ever since then, Dunn's moment of cheeky rebellion has been Exhibit A in countless attempts to explain why smart, independent women are so hopeless at relationships. (The phrase is often falsely attributed to Gloria Steinem, who has corrected the error several times.) Like *Free to Be You and Me* and bra burning (which never actually happened,* but whatever), the bicycle-riding fish makes a handy cultural shorthand to explain how feminism has messed up women's love lives.

Most everyone agrees that it's great that women now can attend college and own property and run for Congress. We can venture into the world on our own, pursue intellectually demanding careers, forge our own identities, and hold out for true love. There's just one teensy catch: We've seriously botched our chances of getting married.

In decades past, the task of telling ambitious women that they'd never find love fell to male editors and reporters, who were unabashed in their contempt for a new breed of she-monster known as the "career woman." Later, the media let the numbers do the talking, and we got clinical analyses likening our odds of marrying to getting killed by terrorists (a particularly chilling analogy, in hindsight). These days it's a woman's job to break the bad news, and often the messenger is single herself, offering up her life as a cautionary tale for the good of womankind.

Regardless of the delivery system, the "doomed career

---

* Bras, girdles, high heels, and cosmetics were tossed into a garbage bin at a 1968 Miss America protest, but no fires were lit.

woman" narrative is as perennial as any Disney fable, the theme repackaged and resold to each generation.

Of course, the astute reader will note that the terrorist statistic isn't true. Susan Faludi's *Backlash* told us so. And twenty years after the fact, *Newsweek* apologized for telling college-educated women they had almost no chance of marrying after forty, explaining that the study they cited was wrong because it used past data to make future predictions, never accounting for the changing shifts in marriage patterns over the last several decades—who could have known women in 2006 would behave very differently than women in 1966? "Such unexpected shifts are part of what makes demographic forecasting extremely difficult, not unlike making weather forecasts in the midst of a hurricane," the editors said.

Husband shortages have another thing in common with hurricanes: There's always another one coming. No matter what women's economic and educational gains, someone invariably finds a fresh algorithm to explain anew why smart, independent ladies who wish to wed are screwed.

There's one problem with all this: It's not true.

Actually, women with college degrees are *more* likely to marry than their less-educated peers—and less likely to divorce. Graduate degrees and high salaries also don't hinder a woman's chance of walking down the aisle. Sociologist Christine Whelan found that women aged thirty to forty-four earning more than one hundred thousand dollars per year are—once again—*more* likely to be married than their lower-earning cohorts.

Women are often advised that the best strategy for ensuring lifelong happiness is to snare a man while they're in school and marry shortly after graduation. But this den-mother wisdom flies in the face of marriage and divorce statistics. The reality is, the older the bride, the stronger the marriage.

Economist Dana Rotz, a researcher at Mathematica Policy Research, found that for every year a woman waits to marry, she lowers her risk of divorce. A woman who marries for the first time in her late twenties (twenty-seven to twenty-nine) is 15 percent less likely to divorce in a given year than a woman who marries in her mid-twenties. If she waits until her early thirties (thirty to thirty-four) that risk drops by another 15 percent. "Marriages made when a woman is in her late thirties (thirty-five to thirty-nine) are more stable still, and fully 46 percent less likely to end in divorce than those beginning when a woman is twenty-three to twenty-six. Up until your early forties, waiting to marry is associated with lower risk of divorce," she told me.

Rotz notes that the trend could very well continue for women who marry *after* forty, but researchers don't yet have a large enough sample size to study it. "Even though marriage after forty isn't that uncommon these days, we need people to have been married a while back in our data so we know if they divorce. Since later marriages are only now becoming common, we just don't have the data to know what's going on," said Rotz, who conducted this research while obtaining her PhD in economics at Harvard.

I'll repeat this happy news, since it's not exactly the message we ladies have received lo these many years: If you get a good education and take time to establish your career and your life as a self-supporting adult, current research shows that you're not only more likely to marry, you're more likely to *stay* married. Oh, and you'll make more money too.

So why are so many media professionals and policy wonks perpetually convinced that a sharp mind and an independent spirit will ruin a gal's chance of finding love? "Because it used to be true," said family historian Stephanie Coontz.

For a long time, having an education *did* correlate poorly with a woman's chance of marrying. "It *truly* used to be good advice for a woman to 'play dumb' to catch a man. Not anymore. Women used to be attracted to older, powerful men who earned more money than they did. That is no longer the case," Coontz wrote in *Marriage, a History*. "Yet many people still plan their personal lives and policy makers still draw up social policies on the basis of these and other outmoded assumptions."

We also unwittingly reinforce them. We're so accustomed to viewing professional and personal success as a binary that "focusing on my career" becomes the default answer for singles asked to explain their relationship status.

You know how it goes. You're at a wedding or a business luncheon and the person sitting next to you asks if you're married, and you say no.

Then there is that . . . gap. So you fill it in: "My work keeps me so busy. I haven't even had time to think about dating" or some such.

You say it because it's true—work *has* been busy. But, more important, because now is not the time to talk about the many complicated factors that led to you being an unmarried thirty-six-year-old. Now is the time to talk about the price of the euro, or your competitor's new branding strategy. You aren't steering the conversation away from your personal life because it's so dark and disturbing—you're doing it because you're a grown-up.

Unfortunately, all this social intelligence has been wildly misunderstood. We have, apparently, left many people with the impression that we're mapping our personal lives with the same precision that we plot our careers—that we're "putting off" marriage, as if falling in love was something you could plan. As if we were gazing at our misty-eyed suitors and saying, "You're amazing and I love you madly. But I'm focusing on my career right now. Sucks about the timing, but what can you do?"

Of course, people do say things like this during breakups. "I just don't have time for a relationship right now" is a perennial among both men and women. And sometimes we even believe it ourselves—because for whatever reason working late on that marketing report *is* more compelling than having dinner with Todd.

But that doesn't mean you're overly obsessed with your career—it probably means you're just not that into Todd. You don't break up with someone you love because "work is crazy." When you're in love, you steal whatever precious moments you can. You drive them to the airport so you can have that time on the freeway together. You make out on street corners before dashing back to the office. You have the company car take you straight to their apartment at eleven p.m., and then have it pick you up from there at five a.m. Friends and family are neglected. Houseplants wither and die. Bills go unpaid; dishes unwashed. But you find time for each other.

Feminism's perpetual PR problem is, paradoxically, rooted in its success. The fundamental notion that women should have equal rights and opportunities was absorbed into the mainstream culture so quickly that we assume it was always thus. It's easy to forget that as late as the 1970s some women were still being told they couldn't get a credit card or buy a car without their husband's permission. When I was a kid in the '70s, the idea that a woman could have an identity that wasn't defined by the man in her life was still new—and still up for debate. So if the fish/bicycle quotation was an awkward overstatement, well, okay. But it was appropriate for the time, and a handy ballast for women in a society that still told them they were nothing without a man.

Feminism never promised women that life would be easy—that there wouldn't be hard choices and massive trade-offs. It never said that the corporate lawyer who hasn't had a weekend off in four months wouldn't at times gaze longingly at the hipster mom knitting a smartphone cozy while her kids play in the park. It merely said she should be free to make her own decisions—and even mistakes—because she's smart enough to find her own way.

Having agency in your life doesn't inhibit your ability to merge it with another's—it only enhances it.

5

YOU'RE TOO INTIMIDATING

Early in her public relations career, Suzanne's boss warned her that her confidence could be intimidating to others. Suzanne appreciated the feedback—she had a good relationship with this boss—but she didn't know how to incorporate it. "Did it mean I had to show a *lack* of confidence? I wasn't sure what to do with that, but it stuck with me for twenty years," she said.

Many years later, as a single-not-by-choice thirtysomething, she continued to hear comments of this nature. Male friends informed her that her self-possession and professional success could be intimidating to guys. Again, this confused Suzanne. She wasn't the CEO of a multinational company or the secretary of state—she was a communications consultant who owned a condo and a few cars, a woman with the self-possession to travel alone or dine in a restaurant by herself.

"My male friends told me that can scare men away, because where is there room for them? They can feel emasculated. They said I needed to look a little vulnerable. I didn't know what that looked like. How do you show someone there is room for them without also coming off as weak and needy?" said Suzanne.

So when Suzanne's then-boyfriend commented that she was unlike the women he usually dated—their appeal being that they let him plan all their dates—she did an experiment. On a bowling outing with a group of friends, she tried to be his kind of girl.

"I decided that I would ask for a lot of advice from him and make sure I wasn't acting too strong. I wasn't acting weak, but I was going to look to him for what would I have—a hotdog or hamburger? I kept getting gutter balls. He responded really well to that."

Others in the group noticed too. "One of the women who was with us said, 'I think Keith is really good for you because you seem more vulnerable with him.' I remember thinking, *So this is what I have to do? I don't know if I can sustain this.*"

The "you're too intimidating" line is a dating-guide staple. And since most intelligent, self-respecting women hear this one at some point, we sometimes take a peek between the pink covers of these books and are thus informed that the qualities that make us successful in life—holding down a job, owning a home, having interests beyond clothing and makeup—can work against us in the dating world. We're also given a strange portrait of men: They're presented as having all the power; at the same time we're told they're hothouse flowers, terrified of any woman who can fix a leaky faucet or unwind a credit-default swap.

Men, these guides explain, need to feel needed. And if you own your own home and dental practice, then what's the point of him? "Regardless of the good intentions of these guides, their underlying message is the social gains women have made in the last few decades cause women to fail in love. They—and here's the real bummer—make women fundamentally *unlovable*," wrote University of Toronto professor Mari Ruti in her delightful book *The Case for Falling in Love*.

Ruti decided to fact-check this assumption that displaying basic competence could make a woman less attractive. So she sent her male friends a one-question survey based on a piece of advice she'd read in a popular dating guide: Would they be turned off if they saw their wife or girlfriend change a lightbulb?

Her friends were baffled—*of course not.* "If a woman revealed to me that she didn't know how to change a lightbulb, this would be a surefire sign that she's a moron. In general, I'm not attracted to morons," wrote one.

"I'm afraid it would be a fairly catastrophic turnoff for me if I found out my girlfriend couldn't change a lightbulb. For me, a huge part of my attraction to a woman is respect and admiration. Competence in anything is one of the biggest turn-ons for me," said another.

Ruti's survey was not scientific. She asked the question in a particular way and sent it to a particular group of guys. She knew ahead of time what their answers would be. This was the point— she replicated the methodology of the dating books she was reading. "Not all men are like my friends. But not all are *unlike* them either. The 'men' you read about in self-help guides—the ones who don't want you to change the lightbulb—are no more representative of 'all men' than are my enlightened friends."

So while you *could* try to act like a nitwit to soothe some dude's fragile ego, Ruti points out that this is rather self-defeating. "You may think that playing helpless will give you a romantic edge. But actually, all it does is to weed out the egalitarian men," she wrote.

Of course, many women have skills that go far beyond performing basic household tasks. They manage large staffs, argue precedent-building court cases, perform open-heart surgeries. These high-powered—and even medium-powered—single women are routinely told that the qualities that make them so successful at their jobs will work against them in their love lives. They are thus advised to develop completely different alter egos for when they leave the office.

This theory assumes, however, that all women with thriving careers have ultra-macho work personalities—that they've gotten ahead by being hard, mean, or aggressive. But is that true?

Think about the most successful people you know—male and female. Sure there are probably some arrogant jerks in there. The history of business shows us a long succession of people who have become extremely wealthy by operating with a soulless disregard for the needs and feelings of others.

But is that how the majority of successful professionals act?

Think about the best boss you ever had—the one you'd work Saturdays for, the one who could make you feel valued even as she told you no one was getting raises this year. Was she cold and impersonal? Did she make others feel belittled and unnecessary?

Or did she understand—as all good managers do—that you inspire a lot more loyalty and hard work in your employees by letting them know how essential they are. Truly successful people know that praise, appreciation, and statements like "What on earth would I do without you?" are far superior strategies for managing a staff than pretending you're all-powerful. So if your career is flourishing, wouldn't that actually speak *well* for your interpersonal skills?

We *all* want to feel needed, and we also all want to be with people who can manage on their own, if need be. So how do you separate that?

How about asking yourself if you've ever looked at a coworker, friend, or relative and truthfully said any of the following:

"Thank you so much for your help. I couldn't have done this without you."

"Do you understand this software? I've been at this for twenty minutes and keep getting error messages."

"Hey, could you grab the other end of this table? It's too heavy for me to lift by myself."

In other words, have you ever looked at another human being and said, "You have skills and strengths that I don't have, because I'm not 100 percent perfect at everything, so I was wondering if you could give me a hand?"

So had Suzanne. And she ultimately married a man with the confidence to let her pick her own damn sandwich.

6

YOU'RE TOO DESPERATE

It was late December, and I was complaining to a married friend about having to spend yet another holiday season without a partner. Understandably, he became impatient: "Sara, in almost every way you have it completely together, but on this one topic you turn into this ridiculous *girl*," he said.

Marriage and family are eternally celebrated as one of the most important and cherished parts of life—for those who have it. But the single woman who says, "Yes, I'd like that too," is immediately dismissed as silly and sad. The fact that you want love is taken as evidence that you're not ready for it.

The other side of single shaming is the complete opposite of the you're-too-independent-and-thus-not-a-real-woman line.

Here any show of wistfulness means you're sort of a twit, a shallow bubblehead with few concerns beyond shopping, pedicures, and "Will he call?" My single friends and I had no interest in shopping or pedicures, but we were wildly embarrassed that we longed for love.

That's why I worked so hard to live up to the "Single and Loving It!" ideal. *Hey, check out my adorable apartment! My fulfilling career! My brilliant friends! Yep, I'm having a blast—no man needed here!* (Though, as discussed, I also knew I couldn't play that card too often, lest the Greek chorus conclude that my well-oiled life left no room for love.)

I wasn't lying. Most of the time I *was* happy—or happy enough. Actually, most of the time, I wasn't thinking about where I fell on the well-being scale—I was just living my life. I had magazine deadlines, editors' meetings, dinner plans. I had a home that needed cleaning and a dog that needed feeding. Like everyone else.

But there were those nights—those cold, January Saturday nights—when I'd gaze at the snow-covered streets, contemplating this solitary life I didn't chose. I didn't need an invitation to a glittery party or reservations at a hot restaurant—I don't even *like* hot restaurants. I just wanted someone to sit next to me on the couch and watch bad reality TV. Someone who would split a six-pack and an order of pad Thai and wonder aloud if Kayla would finally get her comeuppance. I just wanted a damn husband.

This made me feel awful. Admitting I wanted a husband—that I was in fact quite distraught that I didn't have one—made me feel like I was letting myself down, like I was letting *all* of womankind down. Not that any actual feminists suggested it was wrong to want a partner—the emails I received from Planned Parenthood and NOW never took a stand on whether or not it was shameful to want lifelong companionship. No, it was the never-ending cultural debate about whether women's relatively newfound independence was truly making us happy. Funny, isn't it? Freedom is arguably our country's most sacrosanct value—unless we're talking about *women's* liberation. Then suddenly we become cold rationalists, debating pros and cons like a Soviet-era dictator.

Of course, I have no wish to return to the days when single people were necessarily assumed to be miserable, when an unmarried person was an object of pity at best, suspicion at worst. And I certainly know there are plenty of people who genuinely adore their solo life—the freedom, the travel, the deep peace that comes from living in a home where everything is arranged exactly as you like it. But I never did, and this failure became one more bullet point on the list of What Was Wrong.

But what, exactly, was I so ashamed of? Why did I feel like

my deep longing for romantic love made me a nitwit, as opposed to a human being feeling one of life's most natural desires?

"Our need for someone to share our lives with is part of our genetic makeup and has nothing to do with how much we love ourselves or how fulfilled we feel on our own," wrote Amir Levine, a psychiatrist and neuroscientist at New York-Presbyterian Hospital, in his book *Attached*, which he coauthored with Rachel Heller.

If you're single and feel a void—if you find that career, friends, books, and travel are actually *not* enough—it's not because you're dizzy-brained or immature; it's because you're feeling a very legitimate need. "We live in a culture that seems to scorn basic needs for intimacy, closeness, and especially dependency, while exalting independence. We tend to accept this attitude as truth—to our detriment," wrote Levine and Heller.

Of course, this sense of connection doesn't necessarily have to come from a romantic partnership—and many singles rightly bristle at the implication that being uncoupled means they lack strong emotional ties.

Agreed. The problem is that our society is structured around couples and families—and if you don't fit neatly into one of those units, you often have to build a support system from scratch, which is a big task. Friends move, or marry, or disappear into time-sucking work projects. And they usually don't consult you about it.

This all might seem quite dire. *Honey, if you're miserable, well, science says you have good reason.* It could be taken as another excuse to curl up on the couch or frantically fire up OkCupid.

Of course, all of us, no matter what our circumstances, will do best to accept and appreciate our lives for what they are—whether we have companionship at the moment or not. But sometimes we can't. Sometimes loneliness, depression, frustration get the better of us. Sometimes that brutal rejection cannot be shaken off with a Pilates class or an ice cream cone. Sometimes we feel very intense pain.

What I gradually learned was—that's okay. In fact, that dark, Saturday-night despair is what ultimately led me to a new way of relating to pain, one that would serve me for the rest of my life, single or no.

I'll explain that in the next chapter, but for now let's take another look at that awful word "desperate." As Stephanie Coontz points out, the fact that we throw this label on women who have refrained from marrying is absurd. "It's understandable that many women are anxious about the prospect of finding a good husband," Coontz wrote in *Marriage, a History.* "But few modern women are actually *desperate* to marry. Historically, desperate is agreeing to marry a much older man whom you find physically repulsive. Desperate is closing your eyes to prostitutes and mistresses and praying you don't get a venereal disease. Desperate is having child after child because your husband won't let you use birth control or covering the bruises you got last night when you hurry to the market to shop for the evening meal. Women today may be anxious about finding a mate, but most could not even imagine being that desperate."

You *didn't* rush back to that mediocre relationship. You *didn't* grit your teeth and enter some passionless union with a perfectly nice guy who doesn't get you. There *are* people who are afraid to be alone, who head for the nearest warm body after each breakup, or who stay in miserable relationships because the alternative is so terrifying. But that's not you, is it?

7

YOU NEED TO BE
HAPPY ALONE

People like Sheba think that they know what it's like to be lonely. They cast their minds back to the time when they broke up with a boyfriend in 1975 and endured a whole month before meeting someone new. . . . But about the drip, drip of long-haul, no-end-in-sight solitude, they know nothing. . . . They don't know what it is to be so chronically untouched that the accidental brush of a bus conductor's hand on your shoulder sends a jolt of longing straight to your groin. I have sat on park benches and trains and schoolroom chairs, feeling the great store of unused, objectless love sitting in my belly like a stone until I was sure I would cry out and fall, flailing to the ground. About all of this, Sheba and her like have no clue.

That's a quote from Zoë Heller's bestselling novel, *What Was She Thinking? Notes on a Scandal*. Several years after it was published, I interviewed Heller and began reciting that passage.

"That gets quoted back to me more than anything I've ever written," Heller said. She also noted that it elicited a prurient fascination: How would *she* know about this? "There is such a stigma to loneliness. It was as if I had written about having a venereal disease in great detail."

After my *Times* essay came out, women from across the country wrote me confessing their secret shame: Although they told friends and family they loved their solo life, in truth they were lonely.

It's curious: People talk openly about their alcoholism, depression, eating disorders, and sex addictions. But who besides widows of long and happy marriages admits to being lonely? It's the ultimate shame.

The strangest part: Loneliness is *not* a pathology. University of Chicago neuroscientist John Cacioppo explains in his book (cowritten with William Patrick) *Loneliness: Human Nature and the Need for Social Connection* that loneliness is akin to hunger or thirst—it's a natural human response that simply indicates that one needs nourishment.

Loneliness is treated like the ultimate taboo; at the same time, it's regarded as a trifle. That to be a thirty-seven-year-old who has spent a decade without someone to hold her hand at the doctor's office is akin to being a thirteen-year-old sighing over a boy band.

Again, I know—"single" is not a synonym for "lonely." I know there are many lonely married people, as well as lots of single people who have a rich network of deep social connections—friends, sisters, daughters, nephews, etc.—whose lives are as far from Heller's unhappy narrator as can be.

But for many of us, living alone in a society that is so rigorously constructed around couples and nuclear families *is* hard on the soul. What's important to know is that those pangs you feel as you walk though the park, past the multifamily picnics and couples marching by two-by-two, are *not* a sign that you're deficient—they're a sign that you have a functioning internal alarm system.

Isolation, Cacioppo explains, used to be deadly. You needed a close-knit community to protect you from animals, intruders, starvation. Living alone is no longer life-threatening (though loneliness can have a deleterious effect on health). You can live in your one-bedroom and move up in your job and visit your nieces and have a long and productive life. But your biological wiring doesn't know that, which is why loneliness can bring on so much psychic pain.

For me, that pain was at times unbearable—the cold Saturday nights, the summer weekends when everyone I knew had fled the city, the damn holidays. But in hindsight, I realize that learning to manage it was one of the most valuable things I've ever done.

It began, as so many single-woman tales do, in a yoga class. I was on the cusp of a big birthday and was feeling that the end was near—if I'd had a hard time finding a relationship before, it certainly wasn't going to be easier once the clock struck thirty-five. A friend and I had started quoting Porky Pig, "Th-th-th-that's all, folks!" My mind was a steady thought stream of how very screwed I was.

The teacher, an interfaith minister named Frank Jude Boccio, instructed us to do a basic butterfly pose—knees bent, soles of the feet pressed together—and told us to lean forward and get our legs as close to the floor as possible. "Some of you might be feeling some sensation in your thighs right now," he said. "I'd like to suggest that you not label that as pain but simply allow yourself to feel it without judgment."

Immediately, I understood. If I didn't resist the burning sensation, if I simply allowed that feeling to exist without adding the thought of "Ugh, I hate this. When are we going to stop?" it wasn't that bad. The problem wasn't the pain. It was the thoughts around the pain.

At the end of class, Frank asked us to reflect on something that was causing us emotional distress and pay attention to how it felt in our bodies. He then suggested we treat that feeling with the same neutral curiosity that we had earlier applied to the sensation in our thighs.

This was my first introduction to mindfulness meditation, a coping strategy that is not just taught by mystics and yoga teachers, but also some of the country's best hospitals, such as Sloan-Kettering, the Mayo Clinic, and the University of Massachusetts, which pioneered the use of mindfulness-based approaches in mainstream medicine.

I signed up for Frank's meditation class and quickly realized that the pain I experienced on those bleak winter nights wasn't just loneliness. I was piling on a lot of judgment too. Feeling lonely made me feel like a loser, a failure, an outcast. By adding those feelings of shame, I doubled, tripled, or even quadrupled my pain.

Many people think meditating is about not thinking. Actually, the real work of meditating is noticing those thoughts, taking a step back, and analyzing the mind's soundtrack. My inner dialogue, I quickly realized, went something like this: "Why is my life like this? When are things going to change? Why can't I find someone? Why can't I learn to be happy alone? Meghan is single too but she likes her freedom. Why can't I be like that? What's wrong with me?" Lather, rinse, repeat.

As Buddhist nun Pema Chödrön has said, I was "trying to put out the fire with kerosene." I turned that Bunsen burner flame into an inferno.

Gradually, I learned to stick with the original hurt: simple loneliness. I learned to say "I feel lonely right now. That's okay. Everyone feels lonely sometimes." I started to regard the clench in my chest for what it was: a neutral sensation that passed, just something that happens to people, like the flu. I treated my discomfort the way an athlete does, feeling the burn.

Now, sitting at home and feeling pain is, admittedly, not the Saturday night anyone would choose. And of course it did nothing to solve the logistical problem of my isolation. The phone didn't suddenly ring with a stunning invitation or news that the guy I was pining for had asked for my email. The streets outside remained icy and black. But when I stopped feeding the fire—"Why didn't he call?" "Why am I such a loser?"—it very slowly sputtered out.

8

YOU'RE TOO PICKY

Several years ago, my friend Caitlin went on a date with a man who ordered a Shirley Temple. The guy was perfectly nice, but the date was unmemorable, save for the little-girl cocktail. Caitlin thought it was a funny detail, and she shared it with a friend.

Her friend exploded. "He could be the love of your life! And you're getting mad about the Shirley Temple!" she said.

Naturally, Caitlin felt awful. She thought she was telling another goofy tale from the dating trenches; instead, it had become an indictment of her ability to choose a mate. Here was one more piece of evidence that she was hopeless, that her pathological pickiness would prevent her from ever finding love.

You're. Too. Picky. When I asked women what their friends

and family said about why they were alone, this was the overwhelming favorite. It's a nice fail-safe, since it's pretty hard to prove wrong. Maybe he was dull or full of himself last night, but he could be fascinating tonight. If he was rude to the waitress, maybe he was having a bad day. *Give him another chance! Give him another chance!* is the cry of the reasonable.

"So you want me to settle?" I once said testily to a friend. "Is that what you did?"

"Well, no," she said, carefully. "But I did give certain things up."

The implicit assumption—that I wanted perfection or nothing—infuriated me because I wasn't entirely sure it was wrong. How could I be? I had failed my entire life to find this relationship.

To ease the tension, married people counseling singles on this score often divulge the ways in which their own mate falls short of the ideal. The flawed mortals they married are slobs (or obsessive neatniks); they aren't funny (or can't cut the clowning and be serious for once!); they don't appreciate foreign films (or won't shut up about the cinematography in the pretentious piece of crap they made them sit through). The point is, their spouses aren't perfect and if you're looking for perfection, well, good luck with that, sister.

My single friends and I would puzzle over this—*were* our standards too exacting? None of us had salary requirements—we weren't looking for men to support us, though they did need to support *themselves*. Some women wanted guys who were taller than they were; others didn't care. Some felt it was important to share similar political beliefs with their spouse; others . . . didn't. But even these points, we agreed, were subject to be cast aside were we to fall in love.

In fact, we often got the completely contradictory feedback that we were being *too* vague. You have to know what you want! This is achieved by making a list of our would-be husbands' qualities—liking nature, being good with kids, etc. Because how can you find him if you don't know who he is? But be open!

The only standard that truly mattered to any woman I knew was the one articulated by Caitlin: "I want to find a guy who delights and surprises me as much as my friends do, but I also want to make out with." I have yet to meet a happily married person whose spouse fails to clear this bar.

When our friends tell us we're too picky, they're usually responding to a specific detail—the Shirley Temple—but we all know that's not the real reason a particular date is a nonstarter. What really happens is you go on the date and the guy is fine— he asks you thoughtful questions and doesn't make a fuss when the waiter messes up his drink order—but for whatever reason you're not feeling it. Then he starts making a weird popping sound or drumming the table with his fork and spoon, and this becomes the detail you share with your friends. The problem is that there's no chemistry, but your friends hear only about the fork-drumming—hence, you're too picky.

Caitlin married a year before I did—to a terrific guy. But during our single years, this made us nuts—the rolled eyes, the shaking heads, the plaintive questions. "Are you *sure*? Why not just go on one more date?"

Here's what we failed to see: Our friends weren't trying to make us feel bad. They were just trying to help. They were throwing darts at the problem, and in their minds "you're too picky" was the most logical conclusion. After all, accusing a single person of being too selective is a compliment in its way. It's working with the assumption that scads of people *want* to be with you, which is certainly better than saying you need to lose twenty pounds or smile more.

There's another reason we got so much feedback: We asked for it. Or complained vehemently enough that our friends felt compelled to cough up some sort of freelance wisdom.

The solution, once I had the presence of mind to figure it out, was easy: Stop talking about it. If I suspected that a friend's response to a failed five-day romance would annoy me I . . . *didn't tell her.*

Keeping the subject off my single-lady woes was a snap—it turned out my friends weren't nearly as interested in my romantic failures as I'd assumed. And when I forced myself to talk about other stuff—say, the latest Lorrie Moore novel or presidential debate—then I was thinking about *that*; the cryptic email from last night's Internet date faded from my thoughts.

Keeping quiet about my dating life also meant I had to rely on my own judgment rather than a survey of my twelve closest girlfriends, a move that proved extremely liberating. You don't have to justify why you didn't go on that third Internet date if no one knows about the first one.

Did my friends and I make mistakes when we were single? Probably. Did we arrogantly dismiss men who could have turned out to be great husbands for us? Could be. Nevertheless, I'm glad I did *not* take the advice of the acquaintance who said, "You select a husband the way you do a house. You choose from what's available at the time."

Human beings are not houses—you don't walk in and say, "Well, so long as we gut the kitchen and add a third bathroom, this could work," or, "It has no charm, but it's close to work and it's all I can afford." No. You love them as they are, or you let them find someone else who does.

9

YOU'RE TOO AVAILABLE

Rose's relationships usually didn't last long; apart from one three-year romance, most endured for about three to six months. She frequently asked her married friends for advice. "I used to look at married people and wonder about them. I took their advice as golden because they got married," said Rose.

The diagnosis: "There was a general consensus that I was caring too much, not playing hard to get, trying too hard," said Rose.

Rose often became distraught when her relationships ended, and many of her friends quickly lost patience with this. Their advice was tinged with annoyance that she would be so emotional over something that lasted only a few months (apparently not realizing that when your relationships rarely endure longer than a baseball season, it can get pretty upsetting). "There was a lot of advice that basically said, 'What's your problem? Why can't you get out of this?' It had this disparaging 'and P.S. you're crazy' tone to it," she said.

Rose's friends were dispensing fairly classic dating-guide advice: If you love someone, don't you dare let them know. A woman shouldn't be too independent or intimidating, but she also can't be too nice. She's got to play it cool. Keep him guessing. Because men love the hunt.

Even if you've never picked up one of those dating guides that wildly overgeneralize male and female behavior with weird analogies—Men are like cheesecake! Women are like Allen wrenches!—the prescriptions in them are so steeped in our culture that even the most self-help-eschewing single women are well versed in their principles. At many of my single-lady roundtables, women with master's degrees and executive positions would reluctantly agree that asking a guy for a first date was killing the relationship before it started, that you had to make him pay, and that asking the question "Where is this relationship going?" means it's now going straight to hell.

We agreed, to a certain extent, that we were bait, and if we wanted to keep him interested we'd have to zig and zag like a cat toy on a string. Most important, we could never, ever let him know how much we liked him.

We hated those books, but we also believed that we were

rolling the dice when we accepted a Saturday date after Wednesday.

I mostly received the dating-guide wisdom through this kind of osmosis; some part of me knew that actually reading them would corrode my soul. So it's peculiar to read them for the first time after you've already "snared" the guy. How did I possibly pull this off? I made such mistakes as:

- Unlocking his side of the car door after he let me in the passenger side. Apparently, I was supposed to sit there like a princess while he fumbled with his keys. By leaning two inches in and flipping the lock, I was denying him the pleasure of taking care of me. (Driving me someplace apparently wasn't enough.) *Mars and Venus on a Date.*

- Cooking a nice meal for him on the third date. Turns out, I was supposed to toss him a bag of microwave popcorn with an Oreo chaser. The fact that I cooked a proper dinner and offered such niceties as napkins and a glass for his beer meant I was trying *way too hard* to please him and would thus be taken for granted. *Why Men Love Bitches.*

- Hanging out with him for seven nights straight after our first date. *Every dating guide ever written.*

I've picked some howlers, but the essential message—keep him at arm's length, don't let him know you care—was one that my friends and I absorbed without ever opening these books. (Okay, maybe we opened one or two.)

The idea is presented as empowering—to show an image of such supreme confidence that you have no need to prove yourself or gain his approval. Your self-esteem is so sky-high, you're completely invulnerable to his opinion.

As with so much bad advice, there's a kernel of wisdom in there: Don't let another person determine your worth.

But in telling women to behave like ice queens, the underlying message is: *You must hide your true feelings and play-act at being someone else, because if they see who you really are and know how you really feel, they will leave.*

So how is *that* supposed to make you feel confident?

Bitchiness is false confidence. Puffing yourself up, making another person feel insecure, withholding kindness—this is not the way truly confident people behave.

Think about the most self-assured people you know. Are they inconsiderate, selfish, or withholding? Do they try to make you feel small and powerless? Or are they the ones who offer to take your coat and give you their full attention when you tell them about the book you're reading? Are they the ones who notice when you've done something well and tell you so?

Think about yourself when you're feeling most self-assured—when you've received a promotion or a great compliment or just feel damn good for no particular reason at all. Does this wellspring of self-worth make you aloof or ungracious? Are you compelled to make others feel unsure of themselves? Do you withhold praise and affection? Or are you *more* likely to say, "You look fantastic!" "That presentation was phenomenal." "I got you a coffee, cream, no sugar."

University of Houston research professor Brené Brown has spent the past decade studying the difference between people who have a strong sense of worthiness and those who do not. "There was only one variable that separated them," she said in a 2010 TED talk. "The people who have a strong sense of love and belonging believe they are worthy of love and belonging. That's it."

In her research, Brown dubbed those who had this sense of worthiness "whole-hearted" people, and she noticed one of their key distinguishing character traits was a willingness to be vulnerable. "They fully embraced vulnerability. They believed that what made them vulnerable made them beautiful. They didn't talk about vulnerability being comfortable nor did they really talk about it being excruciating. . . . They just talked about it being necessary. They talked about the willingness to say 'I love you' first, the willingness to do something where there are no guarantees, the willingness to breathe through waiting for the doctor to call after your mammogram, the willingness to invest in a relationship that may or may not work out."

This is not ginned-up male-ego-soothing vulnerability—"Golly, I'm too weak to open this pickle jar!" This is the raw courage it takes to let someone know you care for them, without any assurance that they feel the same way.

Love is risky. It involves emotions we can't control. It makes us feel wild, uncontained. This is a *good* thing, but it's also scary. Dating guides sell because they tell us we can control one of life's most unwieldy forces. And it doesn't matter who you are—bus driver, hairstylist, nuclear physicist—love is the thing that at some point leaves you looking at your hands and thinking, "huh."

It's no surprise that into this vast and terrifying space come formulas and prescriptions. But so often, what this "time-tested" advice really does is make you question your most basic instincts, telling you that to be loved you must act like someone you're not.

This is the exact opposite of how Brown's "whole-hearted" subjects approached their lives. "These folks had, very simply, the courage to be imperfect. They had the compassion to be kind to themselves first and then others—because as it turns out we can't practice compassion with other people if we can't treat ourselves kindly. And the last was they had connection—and this is the hard part—as a result of authenticity. They were willing to let go of who they should be in order to be who they were," said Brown, author of *Daring Greatly* and *The Gifts of Imperfection*.

For all of Rose's frustration and self-doubt, she also had a small but fierce instinct that one day she'd meet someone who wouldn't need to be manipulated into liking her. "Since I was young, I always believed when you met the right person, you would know right away," she said. "I never understood why people dated for four or five years—because what further testing do you need? It was this little bit of instinct that I always held on to but never said out loud because I knew I'd get slammed for it. Your instincts can get pummeled out of you by these external voices."

Rose's instinct was correct. She met her husband when she was thirty-four, and they married a year later. As she looks back on all those nonstarter relationships, she *does* wish she hadn't spent so much energy pining for the ones who got away—"I wish I'd just gone for a run," she said.

But she doesn't think that "caring too much" was the problem. After all, she cares like crazy about her husband—and he's pretty happy about that. This attitude bodes well for the longevity of her marriage, since Dr. Gottman's research shows that showering your spouse with love and affection is far more likely to yield a lasting marriage than being aloof or withholding.

This is just an anecdote—like the other stories in this book, including my own, they don't prove anything. Brown's methodology is scientific; mine is not.

But, as Mari Ruti points out, most dating guides aren't scientific either. Single women are constantly assaulted with stories of other hapless ladies who made "stupid mistakes" and the guy went packing. But it's just as easy to find women who did the exact same things and wound up happily married.

Can you prolong a relationship with an ambivalent dipshit by withdrawing your affection? Very possibly. But why would you want to?

10

YOU DON'T KNOW HOW TO PLAY THE GAME

The media treats dating like a cosmic tennis match—one in which women over thirty are always cast as the losers. We're perpetually warned about our low value in the "marriage market," about the steady stream of twentysomethings our male peers can choose from.

Single men, meanwhile, are the great victors, feasting on their multiple dating options, reveling in their bachelor freedom, getting all that milk for free. They're having the last laugh at feminism. What? You'll sleep with me and I don't have to buy you dinner?! Well, ha-ha, thank you, Gloria Steinem!

And because of this, there is a tendency for a girl to be a bit heavy on the defense. After all, we're the underdogs, the ones charged with guarding those vulnerable fortresses—our dignity, our self-worth, and, you know, that other thing. So sometimes we come into relationships defensive and suspicious, ready to pounce on any perceived infraction.

Has he postponed a dinner date? Failed to call at the appointed time? Spent half a second noticing the twenty-three-year-old waitress? Then, sister, you are outta there. "Anytime a guy doesn't do something 100 percent, you get 'You don't deserve that,'" said Melanie Notkin, founder of Savvy Auntie, an online community for aunts and other women who love kids, and author of a book of the same name.

We're all in favor of walking away from any relationship that, for whatever reason, makes you feel rotten. And I personally have wasted a shocking amount of time making excuses for guys who didn't call me for the simple reason that they didn't want to. Of all the clichés that were hurled at me during my single years, "He's just not that into you" is the one I would have been wisest to heed.

But there's a difference between being clear-eyed and being rigid. By now, we pretty much all disdain those Rules books of the 1990s, with their crass diamond-flashing authors and their questionable marriages (one divorced shortly before the publication of their marriage manual). But we haven't let go of that suspicion—one missed call, one thoughtless remark, one suggestion that you go dutch and see ya!

So you keep him guessing—date like your grandma. But don't be too bitchy or threatening because you'll get slammed for that too. As *Outdated* author Samhita Mukhopadhyay points out, you have to be the right kind of bitch—the kind who demands free dinners and must be booked far in advance. Not the kind who can, say, negotiate a contract or win a political argument. You have to pretend to have power, rather than actually have it.

Not long ago, a television writer posted an infamous blog-turned-book-turned-sitcom-deal, telling women why they weren't married. It was a classic piece of flamebait with mean attention-grabbing bullet points—"You're a Bitch," "You're a Slut," "You're Shallow."

The advice was nothing new, a repackaging of the old saws about not being too picky and not sleeping around. The interesting part was the author's stated qualifications: She had married—and divorced—three times. In other words, the author was an expert, not so much in having a harmonious marriage, but in getting a guy to propose.

This particular writer is an easy target—she set herself up to be and took the outrage she ginned up all the way to the bank. But her attitude reflects the bizarrely acquisitive way we view relationships in this country—one in which spouses are seen as trophies to be bagged and put on a wall, where the goal is to get that rock on your finger and prove just how lovable and sexy you are.

Marriage, we're told, is a "market." Which I guess makes us all "commodities." Thus we're encouraged to "sell ourselves" by keeping up rigorous maintenance standards (remember when painting your toenails was a fun, girly thing to do, instead of required grooming?) and providing the illusion of scarcity ("Gosh, Kyle, I wish you'd called sooner because I'm booked through March!") and to cover up any dings or dents in our personalities with dust ruffles and soft-focus lighting.

Lost in all this defensive dating is the fact that what's ultimately being sought is a loving partnership—by both parties.

Anyone who has ever been in a functioning relationship knows they aren't zero-sum games. Happily married men tend to have happily married wives—and vice versa. Either you both win or you both lose. (And actually, if anyone is to "win" from finding a partner, it's men—health and happiness studies show that men, not women, get the biggest boost from marriage.)

The funny thing is, most guys get that. Sure, there are men who just want to fuck and run, and yes, it can at times be very hard to tell the nice ones from the cads—especially when the cads have a tendency to be awfully cute. Desire scrambles the brain, and calling bullshit on something that's exactly what you want to hear is certainly among life's bigger challenges.

We have all, male or female, been that person who makes excuses for someone who actually wasn't "scared" or "troubled," whose only problem was not liking us all that much. And if the gentle suggestion that you "forget him" is coming from several sources, fine, look at that.

But remember: That creep who screwed you over isn't most guys. Most guys are your coworkers, your brothers, and that sweet man you met for coffee and just didn't click with. Most guys do not view themselves as a prize that you're in a competition for—like you're in an episode of *The Bachelor*, rather than Starbucks. Most guys want what you want: A partner in this confusing life.

How do you know when you're making excuses for a douchebag? When are you being overly harsh about a guy who is just a little forgetful?

For me, the best guide was "how does he make me feel?" Setting aside the whole high of infatuation (a tough order, I know)—is the thoughtless remark an aberration from a guy who genuinely seems into you? Or does it set off alarm bells, compelling you to ramp up the salesmanship because the customer is moving toward the door?

And you know what, maybe you will screw up and completely

misjudge a guy who turns out to be a rat. We are all, married or no, at risk of discovering that the person we chose to love will betray us. So instead of armoring ourselves with commandments about what we will and won't accept, isn't it stronger and braver to go into relationships—and first dates—knowing full well you could get hurt, and that you'll also survive?

11

YOU NEED TO GROW UP

Married people like to say marriage is "work," often with a smug, Protestant pride—as if they were plowing fields all day while their single friends sipped appletinis. When I was single, I bought into this. My life might have been lonely sometimes, but my main activities besides writing were yoga class, Internet dates, and drinks with the girls. At least I didn't have to make dinner for my mother-in-law or shop for drapes.

Except that, of course, I *did* have to shop for drapes—that is, if I wanted to live in a home that had nice window treatments, which I did. Also, dinner didn't just make itself.

One day I was talking to a friend about my IRA. I was thinking I needed to diversify more and find a good bond index.

She shrugged and said she didn't know much about that: Her husband handled the retirement stuff. That's when it hit me: *I do everything.*

I do the cooking, the cleaning, the retirement planning, the tax filing. I got the mortgage and handled the refinance and filled the apartment with furniture and the cupboards with food. By myself. When the pipes break, I call the plumber. When it's time to book a flight, I search for the best fare. When the smoke detector needs a new battery, I haul out the ladder and replace it. And of course when a bill needs paying—mortgage, electricity, health insurance—it's coming out of my bank account.

It's not that any of these things individually was so hard—it was just a lot. And it all had to be done with fewer resources, since my one writer's income was significantly less than any of the two-income households I knew. After Con Ed and Chase Mortgage got their cut, there wasn't much left over for purses and facials. And while I did dine out pretty regularly—because, hell, a girl's gotta leave the house—I couldn't afford to go to the trendy, four-star restaurants my married friends raved about.

A Bureau of Labor Statistics analysis found that most single women's lifestyles are pretty far from their glitzy stereotype. In 2008, the average single women spent about twenty-five hundred dollars on clothing, services, and entertainment. The bulk of her income went to food and shelter, not shoes and sweaters.

So why was I living in the fiction that being single was a zippy joyride, that I was essentially a teenager with a debit card?

If married people could boast that their union was "work," why did I feel sheepish about the fact that managing a solo act is often significantly *more* work?

Don't get me wrong—I certainly understand that *parenthood* can be extraordinarily difficult and time-consuming. But that's a false comparison—we're all aware of the existence of single parents and childless couples. At any rate, some recent surveys indicate that single childless women struggle with work-life balance just as much as mothers do, as reported in the *Wall Street Journal* in a story called "Single and Stepping Off the Fast Track."

After the *Journal* ran this story, I read a piece by a single woman who worried that it would give married people more fodder for pity. That the well-cultivated image of the glamorous jet-setting gal would give way to the miserable workaholic subsisting on tuna fish sandwiches.

But I think we merely have to realize that all of these stereotypes are misleading. Being single can be a blast, *and* it can be a grind. It can be extremely liberating to not have to consult another if you want to, say, move to California or join the Peace Corps. But it can also be very stressful to negotiate a home sale or navigate a foreign country without a partner.

Yet single people do this all the time. They buy homes, host holiday dinners, teach English in South Korea. Not only do they do this with significantly fewer financial resources than married couples, but they also pay a financial penalty in nearly every facet of our society—car insurance, health insurance, gym memberships, and Social Security—says social psychologist Bella DePaulo, a visiting professor at the University of California and author of *Singlism*. The extra charges of living single can be as high as one million dollars over the course of a woman's life, say Lisa Arnold and Christina Campbell, the founders of Onely .org, who painstakingly crunched the numbers.

DePaulo also points out that the law explicitly discriminates against single people (which is one reason the LGBT community is fighting for the right to marry). The Family and Medical Leave Act, for example, only entitles spouses, grown children, and parents to take time off to care for a sick loved one. If a childless single person falls ill, only her parents have the legal right to take off work to care for her. If they're deceased or not up to the task, she's out of luck. Even if she has a sister, niece, or best friend willing to take a leave, they won't be legally entitled to do so. *No one* has the right to care for her.

The point here is not to be dreary or give your married friends more reasons to feel sorry for you. It's to respect the fact that you're making it work even though you're operating at a considerable disadvantage.

I'm not saying marriage is always easier. I will grant that being married to a louse who is incapable of emptying the dishwasher—as many people no doubt are—is quite labor intensive.

But that's why a girl must be picky. Being married to the wrong person is work. Being married to an asshole is work. And no doubt sharing a life with the guy you "settled for" is most certainly a challenge—especially once he figures out that your union was motivated more by fear than love.

But you know what happens when you hold out for a kind and considerate human being whom you adore and respect? When you wait until you've already grown up yourself before merging your life with another's? When I talk to late-in-life brides, most report that marriage is . . . not so much work. Sure, there can be fights or conflicts. But it's still a cushy desk job compared to being single.

And in many ways, marriage offers a number of opportunities to lapse, at least temporarily, back into the role of a child.

Whenever Mark and I rent a vacation home, we get a detailed instruction sheet about how to open and close up house—heat, electricity, water, etc. I have never read one of these—I just blindly hand it over and everything is taken care of. (He also is the one who figures out how to get there and drives the car that takes us there.)

This is not retro-style surrendering to marriage, letting him be the Head of the Household. I pull my freight in different ways—when we sold our apartment and bought a house, I was the one who spoke to the Realtors and lawyers and handled most of the paperwork. (And since the apartment was purchased when

I was single, I was the only legal owner.) At times Mark felt bad about this, but that's just how it is in a marriage; you can remain completely innocent of some of the basic facts of your existence and still get full credit for being an adult—*more* credit than if you were handling everything on your own.

Now I see that all those years alone forced me to develop muscles that I never would have fired if I'd married at twenty-six (and which, quite honestly, are in danger of atrophying). In many ways, I was never more adult than I was when I was single.

12

YOU'RE TOO SELFISH

After the 2012 election, some Fox News commentators discussed why single women overwhelmingly voted Democratic rather than Republican. Their conclusion: Married women are more concerned about the future of our country. "Married women tend to be more settled, you're thinking about the kids, thinking about how the country is going to be when they grow up," said one.

Single women, on the other hand, care mainly about abortion and getting help from the government for "health care," one said, using derisive finger quotes.

Slutty, selfish government moochers. Most Americans' views of single women aren't quite as colorful as that, but the idea that the solo life is shallow and insular, that singles never contemplate the world beyond their pedicures while the married folk are out building communities, is hardly limited to conservative news pundits.

Sociologists Naomi Gerstel and Natalia Sarkisian made a very different discovery. After analyzing data from the National Survey of Families and Households and the General Social Survey, they uncovered some surprising findings: Single people devote more time to their extended family, friends, and communities than their married cohorts.

Single women and men are more likely to call, visit, and help out their aging parents with daily tasks (doing housework, driving to the doctor's, etc.) than their married peers. Contrary to the popular image of the lonely social outcast, singles also have more friends than married people, and they take better care of them—calling and visiting more often and offering more practical support with household chores, etc. Single people are also more likely to lend a hand to neighbors and siblings. And never-married women attend more political gatherings and sign more petitions than their married cohorts, the authors said in an article called "Marriage: The Good, the Bad, and the Greedy."

When they first looked at the data, Professor Gerstel told me they assumed the discrepancy could be attributed to the fact that married people are more likely to have kids. After all, having young children who need to be fed and bathed is a decent excuse for not making it to your pal's birthday party or poetry reading.

So the authors controlled for parenthood and found that kids were *not* the culprits. In fact, they found the people who are most disconnected from their communities are married non-parents. All those kids' school and extracurricular activities bring couples back into the fold.

Kids were also a major reason, along with church, why married people do have a better track record than singles when it comes to volunteering—all those requests to help with school fund-raisers and coach soccer. The most popular volunteer activities for unmarried Americans, on the other hand, were mentoring and coaching other people's kids, fund-raising for charities, and distributing or serving food. So while we can give the married some halo points for their volunteer record, it's worth noting that raising money for your kid's school band does not reach the same level of altruism as scrubbing pots at a soup kitchen.

The point isn't to pit singles and marrieds in a battle for who is more virtuous. It is simply to take a harder look at the assumptions we make about singles and question what's real and what's something we absorbed from lipstick commercials.

It's also to recognize the essential role singles play in community life. As Eric Klinenberg pointed out in *Going Solo*, single people are simply out in the world more—spending more time than married couples at restaurants, bars, shops, and public events. They're also more likely to take art or music classes. And they're half the population. In 2012, Klinenberg noted, 49 percent of American adults were unmarried, and 28 percent of all U.S. households were occupied by one person (a percentage that has doubled since 1960).

So it's time to shed this notion that singles live on the margins of society, tending to nothing more than their beauty regimens and their cats. Single people aren't on the fringe of society—they *are* society.

13

YOU NEED TO PUT IT OUT TO THE UNIVERSE!

There are women who always seem to fall in love. At garage sales, bus stops, Laundromats. Some are beautiful; others are not. Some are extraordinarily friendly or quick-witted, and some, well . . .

For those of us whose trips to the dry cleaners rarely include anything more thrilling than stain removal, these sorts of women are puzzling. You might not look like a model but you brushed your hair and put on lipstick. And okay, maybe off-the-cuff quips in the DMV line aren't your forte, but still—you're a basically friendly person who knows how to interact with human beings not connected to your phone.

"Put it out to the universe," they will tell you. "Send a

message" that you're in search of a soul mate. (As if the universe were a big call center.) Your very essence will broadcast this as you wait at traffic lights and take out the garbage. But it won't seem desperate or weird as you beam your love-readiness to everyone at the Quick Pick. Just, you know, magnetic.

This sort of advice does seem kinder and more inspiring than the "straighten up and fly right" variety. And more poetic. You can sit on a mountaintop and visualize your soul mate. You can stand on a rocky cliff and toss a bottled message into the torrid sea. You can write deep thoughts into a fabric-covered diary while soaking in a lavender-scented bath.

There's something very exciting and romantic about putting your faith in the universe. It can make you feel less lonely to believe that the cosmos is somehow looking out for you.

And when you're facing down another birthday or New Year's Eve, this kind of thinking is so seductive. I yearned to have one of those meant-to-be stories. *It was the strangest thing. I was driving in my car and something told me I needed to go to the butcher's, which made no sense because I've been vegan for twelve years. . . .*

I wanted that magic story. I wanted that utter certainty that the heavens were looking out for me. That there was a *plan*. A grid. Something. I wanted some force to guide me to the exact right coffee shop, taxi stand, Bed Bath & Beyond line. I wanted to conclude the day with more than a blueberry muffin and some high thread-count sheets.

I'm sure many people have received great benefits from this kind of advice. It can give a sense of control in a chaotic world and could even lead to some nice epiphanies. Maybe quiet reflection has made you see that you need to quit your management consulting job and go to cooking school (or quit your restaurant job and get a business degree). Maybe you realize it's time to weed that toxic friend out of your life. But if you've dragged out the crystals and started exploring your chakras for the express purpose of finding your soul mate, then it's going to be rough if that person doesn't materialize.

Now you're not just alone, you're also out of sync with the universe. And that's sort of heavy.

Especially when people try to cheer you up with their own magical "how we met" stories. They might be encouraging sometimes, but they also beg the question: Why do the universe's elves and fairies keep blowing *you* off? How come every time *you* meet a guy at the supermarket he turns out to live in his mother's basement?

Our culture's fascination with magical thinking, from "everything happens for a reason" to "it always happens when you're not looking," comes from a nice place, but there is something both cruel and softheaded about it.

Cruel because if everything happens for a reason, then what is the *reason* a child is abducted or an oil rig explodes? What is the *reason* one woman "won" her battle with breast cancer while

78

your sister "lost"? Softheaded because it suggests a refusal to face what anyone who has ever opened a newspaper understands— that much of life is arbitrary and unfair.

When I started Internet dating, it felt like defeat. I had failed to meet someone "naturally"; my soul was a dud. This was back when online dating was fairly new, when the phrase "a guy I met on the Internet" made your married friends shudder. When the notion that ex-boyfriends would stumble upon your profile and think *wow, tragic* seemed all too real.

So I braced myself for a miserable slog through all the freaks and weirdos, but discovered something very different. Nice guys. Cute guys. Guys with jobs. Nice, cute guys with jobs who wanted to go on a second date *with me*.

Okay, I know. Internet dating is old news. Now, instead of making your married friends wince, it has become their default cure-all. In the same way infertile couples are informed about adoption—*Wait? Really? There is a system by which people can parent children born to others? Tell me more!*—now singles are routinely informed that you can meet people online.

So sure, you know about Internet dating, you've been doing Internet dating and . . . you're reading this book.

If you've gone the OkCupid route and decided it's not for you, fine. Online dating has worked beautifully for some, not at all for others. (Which I'd wager has more to do with the demographic composition of certain locales, rather than individual personalities.) But here's what we can all appreciate about it: It has given lie to the idea that finding a life partner has anything to do with purifying your soul.

Before Internet dating, it was easy to get sucked into the idea that you could turn yourself into a tuning fork, set your psyche on a particular radio frequency and then he would appear. It was a fun thing to think but it also carried a heavy judgment. Because this philosophy essentially said your married acquaintances found their spouses not because they happened into the right organic chemistry class or bartending job. No, they had more than mere *chance* on their side—they had *the universe*. The universe was grinding on overtime to ensure that all those seemingly fluky occurrences added up to their cozy family of four sitting at the dining room table. And if you could just pull your shit together maybe you could get on the cosmos's GPS.

But there's absolutely nothing soulful or poetic about Internet dating. And yet, it works. Maybe not for you, maybe not yet, but for some people. The least magical, most un-precious way of meeting people is also one of the most effective. One Stanford University study found that online dating has become the second-most common way for couples to meet, and the people who benefit most from this medium are thirty-five to forty-four. And a University of Chicago survey of more than nineteen thousand people who married between 2005 and 2012 indicates that a third of marriages now begin with Internet dating.

In both studies, researchers found that the relationships that began online suffered no penalties in terms of quality or longevity. "We found no differences: romantic relationships originally formed online are no different in quality than any other relationships, and relationships originally formed online are no more fragile than relationships formed offline during a similar period," wrote authors Michael J. Rosenfeld and Reuben J. Thomas. The University of Chicago study found that the marriages that began with online dating were slightly *more* likely to endure. (The U of C study was paid for by the dating site eHarmony, but independently reviewed, and eHarmony agreed upfront that it would be published regardless of the results.)

As of yet, there is no peer-reviewed data on the efficacy of journaling by candlelight.

Not that that isn't a great thing to do. It's wonderful to live in a home with harmoniously arranged furniture and who doesn't like a good soak in a rosemary-water tub? But laying on the extra thing—*I'm doing this so I can find a partner*—will only diminish these pleasures. I say this from personal experience.

Internet dating, like vaccines and eyeglasses, is one more thing that shows us we're not slaves to what "happens naturally." We have brains that develop tools that can counter these things.

More important, we can take a more grown-up approach to life and realize that God or the universe or whatever you choose to call it probably isn't some eternal babysitter doling out goodies and lumps of coal.

You can't control whether that magic person pops into your life, but if you're tired of waiting for fate to stop pressing the snooze button, perhaps there is comfort in the fact that humble tasks like filling out online questionnaires and meeting random strangers for lattes are at least as effective as burning incense and summoning ancient deities.

As for magic, well, here's some. We now have machines that can tell us where to locate other people who are looking for love and might like to date us. We can use those machines to set up appointments, and other machines to get us there.

Hitting the send button might not inspire a sonnet, but it *is* connecting with the universe.

14

YOU NEED AN ACTION PLAN!

We walked into the Manhattan bar, five women in their late thirties.

"See anyone?" one friend said.

We surveyed the room. Some couples, a group of women, a few guys who appeared far more interested in each other than any woman in the room. We shook our heads and moved on.

We repeated this three or four times until finally shoehorning ourselves into a crowded bar where we drank bad merlot and stared into space, waiting for the time when we could go home and catch the Barbara Stanwyck marathon on TCM.

In other words, we were the embodiment of the worst singleton stereotype, a group of lonely, not-young women roaming from bar to bar, scanning each one like a police chief looking for a murder suspect.

But wasn't that what we were supposed to do? Taking action, taking the reins? What would those who scoff have us do? Sit at home in our pajamas with the clicker?

The flip side to the magical-thinking prescription is the advice that tells women to treat the search for a husband with the same laser-pointed focus that you would a job or a cure for Parkinson's. The beauty of this kind of advice is that it gives the illusion of control. You're so busy with your twelve-point action plans and your group strategy sessions that even if you don't find him tonight at least you know you're being a good single-woman citizen. You are applying yourself! You are trying!

Until you find yourself flat-out exhausted from one too many joyless evenings of *searching*. So you say, *you know what, screw this*, and spend the next five Saturday nights in front of the television. If it never happens—well, at least you never had to hang out in a sports bar pretending to be interested in the Stanley Cup.

But eventually, *that* makes you feel bad and you decide to get back "out there." And the whole cycle begins again.

Sure, there are plenty of times when you're in neither extreme—when you're at a rock-climbing class or your nephew's play or playing guitar at your favorite bar's open-mike night. But even then it's hard to dim that flicker of hope—maybe there will be a sweet single dad at the concession stand!—and the subsequent disappointment of *no, not tonight.*

Actively searching can be soul crushing, but as we all know "letting love come naturally"—let it find you at Pilates class or your marketing job—has serious problems too. And no matter what you do, you're always informed that you're wrong, alternately urged to "just relax" or "get out there," depending on whichever thing you're not doing.

So how do you find that razor-thin line, that place where you burst open the doors of your house, take a deep breath, and say, "Hello, world. I'm going to live the hell out of this day, but also be *open to love!*" How do you cultivate that magical energy that people who married at twenty-two were apparently born with, that very particular frequency that radiates both openness to change and complete satisfaction with one's life, with just a little bit of sex appeal?

First, let's dispense with the idea that everyone in a functional relationship has achieved this hallowed state. Witness your friend who met her husband at a frat party at three a.m., after throwing up in a bush.

Still there's an interesting philosophical question in there: How do you find, as the yoga teachers say, the balance between effort and surrender?

I had a chance to ask Buddhist teacher Ciprian Iancu

essentially that question. At a talk, he described a similar kind of night, as he offered the example of being in a bar at two thirty a.m., after you've had too much to drink and the person you have a crush on is not responding the way you'd like.

"Everything stopped being fun hours ago, but you stay, hoping you can suck just a little more fun out of the night," he said.

This, he said, is the classic Buddhist definition of suffering: craving something you can't have.

If you're lucky, something snaps. You get a drink of water, call a cab. You go home. It's not necessarily a *happy* moment, but it is the moment that you reclaim your dignity. It's when you face the hard truth: *Tonight is not the night.* And maybe when you have an even deeper epiphany. *I'm not going to be this person anymore. I'm sick of this shit.*

The Buddhist view is that the cause of suffering is craving and ignorance. You're looking outside of yourself for happiness. You're not okay with the present reality. The path out of suffering is to accept things as they are and to allow whatever pain those circumstances cause you—loneliness, frustration, even self-loathing—to simply be there without judging them. When you start to see these feelings as simple sensations, sensations that will pass, you realize they're manageable. It's the thoughts around them that get us into trouble: *What am I doing in this place where no one looks old enough to drive? Where did I go wrong?* That's the salt that we invariably put in the wound.

"But sometimes it's good to strive for things, right?" I asked Iancu. "You want a new job, so you send out résumés. You want a relationship, so you go out."

"Absolutely," he said. "Buddhism has no problem with going after things. The problem is not in the wanting; the problem is what happens when you don't get what you want." In other words, the problem is not saying "Gee, I hope we meet some cute guys tonight. Let's go to a place where there's a decent chance of that happening." The problem is when we decide that if the evening *doesn't* end with swapped cell-phone numbers or a weird back-alley make-out session, then it is a failure.

So how do you find that line? "Only you can know that," said Iancu.

For me, the strategy was: Does this make me feel empowered or just exhausted? Am I allowing my desire for the evening to go one way to spill into desperation or am I maintaining my dignity?

Dignity is what happens when you don't get sucked into knee-jerk reactions. When you meet your coworker's sexist insult with a quizzical look and return to your work. When you get the *I don't think this is a match* email and take a moment, cry—if that's what's happening—and then write back, *I'm sorry to hear that. Best of luck.* It's not suppressing or denying pain; it's allowing it to be there without embarrassment. Dignity transcends circumstance.

That night when my friends and I roamed from bar to bar was awful. But the problem wasn't that we were searching, or even that we were lonely. The problem was we weren't having any fun. We were trying to force the evening to go one way, and we were caught up in a lot of storylines about why it wasn't.

And that is the best answer I can find to the *how hard should you look* question—as hard as you want to.

My guess is that you're already straddling both worlds—at least insofar as sometimes you're actively searching for a partner, and sometimes you're not. But if you're caught in that seesaw tug—never quite feeling that what you're doing is the "right" thing—that's the part to drop. If you're looking for guys online, look for guys online. You don't need to add the subtext of *God, this is such a lame thing to be doing on a Friday night. I should be out swing dancing.* And if you're swing dancing, swing dance! No need to worry that, despite what your local paper's "Ten Best Places to Meet Singles" story said, the average age in the room is eighty-five.

Now when I remember the woman I was—heaving herself off the couch to go on another Internet date, taking a deep breath before walking into the party where she'd see her ex and his new girlfriend—I don't feel a trace of contempt or embarrassment. I have a funny admiration for the girl who kept taking her licks and got back up again. *That was me. Doing my best.* Which, of course, is all any of us can do.

15

YOU'RE TOO FABULOUS
TO SETTLE DOWN

"Your life sounds so exciting! So glamorous!" the married folk say after you mention you're going to see a movie with a guy you met while getting your car inspected. This is often preceded by one of those "I'm just a boring mom" humblebrags. "And *my* big plans are playing fairy princess with Bella and trying to corral Connor into the tub. . . ."

Not that these comparisons are entirely unwelcome. After all, if you're going to get your second choice in life, might as well *rock it.*

So you play along. Last night's Internet date might have been less-than-bedazzling, but he was a doctor (a dermatologist, but still!) and he had those philharmonic tickets that his coworker abandoned. So you lightly mention the MD and string ensemble because why not? If life and television have given you this little chip, might as well push it to the center of the table. Go ahead: Sprinkle in the names of a few more mystery men—"Matt the investment banker," "Trey the bass guitarist."

"We can't keep them all straight!" they say.

"Me neither!" you cry.

Professional lives can also be goosed up for maximum glam, because as Melanie Notkin points out, all gainfully employed single ladies are "career women." Marriage? Babies? Who can think of such things when you have that quarterly earnings report to file!

And you need to be a "career woman" because how else will you afford the necessary accouterments of a cool singleton's life: the weekends in Paris, the wine-tasting courses, the two-hundred-dollar hair treatments. Not for you the state-park stay-cations and dollar-days coupons. That's just-a-boring-mom's territory!

My profession has always prevented me from having much disposable income, but freelance writers are often paid in rhine-stones and glitter, anyway. So there would be an interview with a famous author, a job reviewing a spa, a launch party where caterers served expensive champagne and pretty little canapés. These became the bright, shiny stones I used to build my armor of fabulousness—pay no attention to the woman eating leftover spaghetti in front of the television. I curated and cherry-picked my life the way one does a Facebook page. I edited myself down to a nice glossy package and said, "This is me."

And a big part of that "me" was the men—because, oh honey, were there men. I quickly realized that the most important thing about being fabulous—more than the professional achievements, or the travel, or the artisanal cocktails—was to make very, very clear that *I didn't need a guy.*

The fact that I had been on my own for many years somehow didn't count. The only way to really prove I didn't *need* a guy was to *have* a guy—and then make clear how unnecessary he was.

Honestly, I wasn't terribly good at this. I had exposed my lonely, throbbing heart too many times to convince anyone that I wasn't interested in a relationship. But once in a while I'd be seeing someone who sounded good on paper—because he had a cool-sounding job or country of origin—but I didn't really connect with beyond the initial physical attraction. I knew something essential was missing below the surface, but I'd let it go because things looked so damn good *above* the surface. An intelligent, good-looking man was buying me dinner; later, we'd go back to my apartment and he would kiss me. Maybe this was all I'd ever get. Maybe this was enough.

I tried to convince myself that feeling detached was a sign of strength—dating like a man and all that. These not-quite relationships also smoothed things over at family gatherings or anywhere else where I might be asked if there was anyone in my life. "I'm seeing an architect right now—it's fun, nothing serious" sounded a whole lot better than "no."

But it often didn't feel so good the morning after one of those just-for-fun dates. There would be that awkward, ambivalent parting ("I'll call you." "Sure, whatever.") and I'd feel momentarily relieved. Then I'd pour myself another cup of coffee and stare out the window, realizing I'd traded in one kind of feeling like shit for another.

So I stopped. Being alone and celibate didn't sound as cool, but at least it was honest. And one of the things I liked best about Internet dating was that, contrary to popular perception, my experience of it was quite chaste. The fact that these men were strangers plucked from the ether—as opposed to friends of friends—meant that everyone understood that sex was a long ways off.

I don't regret any of my quasi relationships—they were where I was at the time, and they were fun for a while. I also understand that many people don't have this issue—that they can enjoy a casual fling without getting broody about it. That's great. If you're having a blast with your sexy European lover—but are also glad he has to be in Madrid every other week—please, don't let me stop you.

I have no problem with being fabulous. My problem comes

when you won't allow yourself to be an ordinary woman with a decent apartment and an okay job. When only the mom is allowed to be boring—because her life is so rich with meaning.

When I carefully choreographed the story of how amazing I was, I was acting like one of those helicopter parents—you know, the ones who refuse to admit that their Jackson might suck at math or Stella might not be the world's greatest violinist. "You are special! You are special!" they cry to their children, hoping this will boost their confidence. But the real message is one of panic: You *must* be special. Ordinary is not okay. When I walked into a party projecting the Shiny Girl—she of the lighthearted flings and glitzy job—I was essentially doing the same thing.

Dropping that bit of performance art meant I could relax and be plain old Sara—the Sara who hadn't had a date in nearly a year, whose working day was spent writing a newsletter for a supermarket chain. This didn't have to be a self-effacing thing—*ha-ha, I'm such a loser*—it meant that I really wasn't regarding myself at all. That I was allowing myself to fade into the background a bit, which strangely enough left me feeling stronger and more confident than when I was giving them the ole razzle-dazzle.

I could also see that friends, my family, the people I met at weddings were never really demanding that I be fabulous. It was just a convenient script, one designed to make everyone more comfortable.

We can't all be fabulous and we can't all be mothers, but we can all have meaningful lives. That will look different to everyone, of course, but one thing is certain: It need not involve chasing naked toddlers around with bath towels, nor does it require a designer-shoe budget.

16

YOU'RE TOO SAD

One of the challenges of telling others that your singlehood is not entirely chosen is that in many people's minds the logical leap from "single and not thrilled about it" to "pathetic" is perilously short. It's just easier to tell everyone how content you are with your kayak and your dog. After all, you *do* get a lot of enjoyment from these things, so why dwell on the part of life that hasn't quite worked out the way you'd hoped?

As you offer these reassuring details to friends and family, they will sometimes ask "Are you happy?"

This is almost always a well-meaning question; it's also quite condescending. Imagine asking a married person if she were happy. It would be wildly inappropriate. Married people are afforded a veil of privacy. We respect that marriage might be hard sometimes but ultimately is worthwhile. When you're married, you're assumed happy unless proven otherwise.

The question of single women's happiness is perpetually debated. Newspapers and magazines are forever pressing over-thirty single women to report on how fulfilled they feel by their jobs, their friendships, their nieces and nephews. The articles are accompanied by pictures of the subjects skydiving or smiling with satisfaction at the mid-century split-level they renovated on their own. (I should know; I've written one or two.) The sidebars are chipper listicles about the great perks of singledom—not having to share the clicker! Cereal for dinner! Woo-hoo!

Again, it is a very, very good thing that singleness is now presented as a valid life choice, one that is often preferable to coupling up. It's certainly an advance from the days when a single woman's misery was a foregone conclusion. But it also poses the question "Are Single Women Happy?" as a subject for debate, one over which there are strongly contrasting points and counterpoints.

Reporters are sent scrambling to get the contrarian voice, and they're easy to find. A call to a conservative think tank will quickly get you connected with a social critic to proffer the needed sound bite about entitled, narcissistic single women doomed to unhappiness. She will warn older singles about the men "looking over their Chardonnays at women in their twenties" (to cite one quote that echoed through my consciousness during my thirties—well done, conservative social critic!).

Marital happiness, however, is still pretty much assumed. But as Bella DePaulo points out, this assumption is problematic, as research "proving" that married people are happier than singles accounts only for the *currently* married, neglecting the roughly 40 percent of people who divorce. "It is like saying the new drug Shamster is very effective, based on a study in which the experiences of nearly half the people were discounted because it most certainly didn't work for them," she wrote.

Popular thinking *has* changed somewhat over the fruits of many of those marriages: children. When studies first began surfacing that said people who have kids are less happy than people who don't have them, childless people responded with glee and parents with outrage. Later, the moms and dads gloated about subsequent studies concluding that parents were the happier group.

It became a war of data, one in which everyone was protesting a bit too much. After all, if you're truly happy, do you really need a study that will show it? Why are we all competing in this battle for happiest of them all, anyway?

For that matter, why is happiness the only marker of success? Why are there never debates and cover stories about who is more compassionate? Who is wiser? Who is more fun to have a beer with?

Judging people based on how happy they are is better than on, say, whether they own a powerboat, but there is something about all this happiness one-upmanship that feels pretty sad.

Because what we're really seeking is assurance that the other gal doesn't have it so great. When I was single, I noticed that when I was out with three or more other unattached women, someone would eventually start discussing the misery of their married friends. This was always a popular topic. When someone piped up that actually their married friends seemed pretty happy, the table got quiet.

Are you happy? If we're honest, the answer for most of us is "sure—sometimes. And sometimes I am sad. Other emotions I feel include: anger, contentment, nervousness, and excitement."

In the Buddhist view, this is as it should be. To try and stamp out one feeling and replace it with another is to deny yourself life. It's like saying I only want to taste sugar, never salt. I only want to see the color blue, never orange.

"A much more interesting, kind, adventurous, and joyful approach to life is to begin to develop our curiosity, not caring whether the object of our inquisitiveness is bitter or sweet," wrote Pema Chödrön in *The Wisdom of No Escape*.

I spent a good portion of my single years falling asleep to Pema's voice—her *Sounds True* recordings gently reminding me each night that I didn't have to play ball with this project of being a perfectly self-actualized single woman. Reminding me again and again and again that longing was not desperation and loneliness was not failure. And that, ironically, the less I tried to manipulate my inner experience, the more peaceful and content I felt.

If you feel sad sometimes, it's not because you're single—it's because you're alive.

17

YOU ARE THE CONSTANT

Caitlin was venting to her friend Dan about her frustration with men—there seemed to be a pattern where she met a guy she liked, they'd date for a while, and then he'd drift away. She expected Dan to shake his head and say, *That's crazy. Why would anyone blow* you *off? You're amazing.* Because that's what people say to their friends, and it's what Caitlin's friends had always said to her. But this time, Dan looked at her gravely and said, "Well, the constant in all these stories is you. Do you think maybe you're the problem?"

"He didn't say it in a mean way," said Caitlin. "But I remember thinking, *Oh my God, the tide is turning.* In your youth, the story is *he's an asshole.* I suddenly very distinctly realized, *Now I'm the marked one.*"

Caitlin didn't feel like anything was wrong with her, at least not yet. "I didn't feel that I had to be something different than I was, but I did have the feeling that people were going to start perceiving me that way: If it didn't work out, I was the constant. After that went on for a bit, of course I started to feel that way too."

You are the common denominator in all your failed or nonstarter relationships. It's another form of circular logic routinely dispensed as tough love.

The math here is pretty easy to break down—obviously anyone who wants but is not in a long-term relationship has not yet succeeded in finding the forever one. But anyone who is *in* a relationship hasn't necessarily found it either. Your nana and your papa celebrating their seventy-fifth anniversary have bragging rights. With anyone else, it's an open question.

Still it can, for the time being at least, appear that some have an easier time of it than others.

So you sit with this fact: *I am the constant.* And you try to figure out what is that *thing* you do *every single time* that either drives them away or else makes you skip town. Are you radiating some kind of buzz-killing neediness, or are you *simply incapable* of true intimacy?

You pore over the evidence, like a fiendish detective who won't quit until the culprit is found (despite the orders of his pragmatic, coffee-mug-wielding boss to "let it go, man"). You stare at the walls papered with newspaper clippings, handwritten notes, and grade-school portraits, thoughtfully distributing pushpins and stringing them together with brightly colored yarn. You are getting to the bottom of this. You are connecting the dots!

And then: Aha! You always get scared about three months in. The men you date are a tad too close to their moms—the last one called her *every* Sunday. You always choose guys with really demanding jobs—well, except for that underemployed bike messenger/stand-up comic or the out-of-work puppeteer. But: Exceptions prove rules!

Gradually, you paste together all these snapshots and start to create a story. Depending on your mood, the story can be good or bad. There's the one about how brave and independent you are, how unlike some wimps you could mention you refuse to settle—go you! Except that you *want* to find someone and, truth be told, actually hate being alone, so then the story becomes about why you're repulsive to prospective partners. Even if you don't diagnose yourself with any of the aforementioned pathologies, it's the story of something *lacking*. Other people must have *that special something*, some secret skill, some dog whistle that makes a substantial portion of the dating pool perk up their ears to her siren song. *I'd cohabitate with that.*

Or maybe you're pretty good at getting to the shopping-together-for-a-sofa part; the only trouble is that at some point custody of said sofa is in dispute. You have serious relationships; it's just that they *always end*. In this case, you're encouraged to feel good about the fact that you're capable of getting to the joint gym-membership stage. You have brought partners home for the holidays and vacationed with them in foreign countries. You have experience. You are *learning*. On the other hand, you always blow it, don't you? So what's up with that?

Again comes the narrative—of the woman who chooses the wrong men, or who bugs out when the going gets tough, or who has the guts to leave while others slog through empty relationships.

Whether you cast yourself as the hero or antihero, the need to create that personal myth is seductive. Because with the story, you might get an explanation. Why is this happening? Why does this *keep* happening?

The problem with stories: They're made up. They're very intricate conjectures on why he said, "Things just aren't clicking for me." With the story, you fill it in: Things weren't clicking for him because I'm too emotionally distant. And I'm too emotionally distant because my dad was never around.

It's not that the story is necessarily wrong. Hell, I don't know, maybe you *are* afraid of commitment. But I noticed that when I stepped back and looked at my own tall tales, the ratio of fanciful assumptions to sober facts was pretty high.

When I let go of the speculation, the only thing I really knew was that the guy who was making out with me on the couch last weekend didn't want to make out on the couch with me anymore.

And that fact, unpleasant as it was, really didn't say anything definitive about me. It was merely a statement of a particular circumstance and while it hurt more than, say, "it snowed last night," it was no more complicated.

The other problem with creating the story of "the woman who attracts the wrong men" or the "guy who deep down doesn't *want* a relationship" is that we tend to share those stories with our friends, who will be equally inclined to latch their brain around an explanation—because they love us, and because they'd like us to shut up already. And thus another unreliable narrator is brought into the fold, analyzing your life through the smoked glass of her own experience. (Don't expect the friend who settled in her own marriage to budge from her "too picky" diagnosis.)

When I squabbled with my pal in Oregon—she of the lake house bungalow and sweet, musician boyfriend—I was completely insufferable, repeating in various ways an incessant mantra of *it's unfair, it's unfair, it's unfair.*

It wasn't until the redeye back to New York—after three hours crunched in the middle seat, staring at the upright tray table—that it hit me. *Oh yeah, it's unfair.*

So I had been unlucky—so what? Why did I need to badger my friends about it? The reason, I realized, was that I desperately wanted their validation. I wanted someone to brush away that nagging doubt—*I am the constant*—and say, "Nonsense. Life is arbitrary. You don't need to do anything different; you don't need to *be* anything different. You just need a little luck."

As I watched the sun rise through the oval window, I realized no one was going to say this to me. But for the first time, it was okay. I finally believed it myself.

The Buddhists say, "Of the two witnesses, hold the principle one." Meaning: You're the only one who knows your experience. As imperfect as our analyses may be—as clouded as they are by judgments, worries, and fantasies—they're still the best we have.

It's great to have loved ones who give us advice, feedback, brownies, alcohol. But we can't expect them to tell us who we are. It's not fair to them and greatly underestimates our own natural intelligence.

You are the only one who knows. You are the constant.

18

YOU HAVE TO KEEP TRYING!

So I declared my self-improvement project complete. I was thirty-six years old. Maybe I'd find someone, maybe not. But whoever he was, he'd have to take me as is.

If my life were a movie, this would be the part where I meet my true love—or, more likely, suddenly develop a wild attraction to the shy computer nerd in the apartment downstairs, the one who'd been there all along.

Instead, my life proceeded pretty much as it had before. I did my work, hung out with friends, occasionally dated. And despite my grand transcontinental epiphany, I still experienced many, many moments of self-doubt.

The outlines of my life remained unchanged, but something

had shifted: I had decided to stop taking my single state personally. I greatly reduced the time I spent fretting about what my life was not and vastly increased the time spent enjoying what it was.

But I was still left with an uncomfortable question: If finding a romantic partnership is largely a matter of chance, how exactly does one face that wildly uncertain future?

One blustery fall night, I was having drinks with a married friend when I mentioned how strange it was to live what often felt like a twenty-five-year-old's life—trying to meet guys, going to my parents' at Christmastime—while most of my peers were preparing their youngest child for the second grade. "I'm trying to figure out how to be in the world as a single person this age. How do I relate to my life knowing I might always be single?"

My friend paused for a second. "Keep moving," she said.

I understood what she meant. If I wasn't content with my life as it was, then I needed to keep trying new things, keep meeting new people. It was advice I had essentially been giving myself for years.

But now it felt off. "Keep moving" felt a little too much like I was running scared, dogged by some toothless sea hag, my future self. Keep the old bat away with artists' colonies and chocolate-tasting classes and glamorous journalism assignments. Don't sit still because where you are is unacceptable.

No, that didn't seem right. Yes, yes, I'd continue to—heavy

sigh—*get out there* in the hopes of raising the odds that I would eventually meet someone.

The problem was the intention behind it, that underlying panic. I needed a way to rest into my single life, without giving up on romantic love.

Because the truth was, many of the things I did in the name of self-improvement *were* making my life better. I used to be a klutz, but after a decade of yoga my foot could fly on a patch of black ice and I'd somehow manage a midair twist and land upright. I used to be capable of spending entire subway rides mentally rehashing some ancient gripe. Meditation had enabled me to short-circuit my thought tirades and do something more productive, like read ads for chemical peels in Spanish. I used to be terrified of public speaking. After a couple years of acting lessons, I stood on a stage in the East Village and told a group of strangers about the mother-daughter sex education class I took when I was ten.

When I was single, it was always New Year's Day. I perpetually hectored myself with resolutions—"Hold a dinner party once a month!" "Write to a new guy on Match twice a week!" But that also meant I was constantly expanding my world.

In short, I did a lot of cool stuff. I pushed myself in a way that I never would have if I'd married by thirty. The problem was, I attached a condition to these experiences. Underneath there was always a niggling voice, one that asked, "Why isn't this working?"

I saw these experiences as building blocks to a single goal, making them part of a cosmic checklist:

✓ Fulfilling career
✓ Giving back
✓ Adventurous
✓ Financially stable
✓ Good friend
✓ Emotionally balanced
✓ Physically fit

Somehow, I believed that by hitting all of these marks, I would one day emerge as a woman capable of a lifelong partnership. Like there was some celestial scorekeeper, some relationship Obi-Wan Kenobi, who would one day nod sagely and say, "Yes, my child. You are ready."

When that didn't happen, I became frustrated and bitter—and extremely ungenerous when others found love.

"That's great!" I'd say with a twitchy smile as they detailed the series of crazy coincidences that led them to their one-and-only. I felt like I was studying extremely hard for an exam, only to see others ace it without cracking a book. And unfortunately,

I allowed this goal-oriented view to siphon the very real happiness I was finding.

Eventually though, I learned to patch that pinhole leak—or at least become attuned to the sound of whistling air before I completely deflated.

Once, for example, I was hanging out in a riverside park with a friend—drinking iced coffees, watching tourists. She mentioned that a woman I vaguely knew was getting married. Immediately, my heart went black. I felt that familiar self-pity—*why is it always someone else?* But this time was different—this time I saw my response from the outside, like I was watching a movie. She hit a nerve. I had a reflex—the kind you have when the doctor taps a rubber mallet on your knee. I saw it, without judgment, and quickly collected my wits. A distant acquaintance was having a wedding. Big deal. We went back to the lovely day.

This isn't about giving up. It's about lightening up. By all means, continue to make your life as rich and interesting as possible. Learn to speak Mandarin, become a Big Sister, take that solo trip to Peru. But do them for their own sake, not as a means of polishing your life résumé or reassuring yourself or the world of your worthiness. You're already worthy. There's nothing to prove.

19

YOU'RE STUCK

Several years ago, a friend was moving when she found a box of old diaries, which started from her middle school years. As she read them over, she noticed a recurring theme—"Will I ever find someone?" There was one exception, the very happy four-year relationship she had in her twenties, one that ended tragically when her boyfriend died in a car crash.

During that period, she found many more entries about philosophy, politics, art, theater. When she told me this, I knew that if I had kept such meticulous track of my own mental gyrations I would have made a similar discovery. It wasn't that "Will I find him?" was my *only* thought. Sure I contemplated the latest Richard Ford novel and campaign-finance reform. I read eight-hundred-word accounts of the Enron scandal and discussed the Senate primaries with my girlfriends over cocktails.

But somewhere in the back of my brain, the question of my singleness was always grinding away, slowing sapping precious mental energy.

I said in Chapter 17 that getting rid of the story is key to cultivating a more peaceful mind, but that's hard to do when distressing thoughts—"Why am I still alone?" "Why didn't he like me?"—keep popping back up.

"You need to get over it," friends and family will say. "You need to get out of your own way." These comments can seem pretty valid, since the truth is you *do* seem to have a lot of soul-sucking thoughts. But the "you're stuck" advice has a false assumption—that the spinning and churning is the *cause* of the problem, rather than a symptom. It assumes that if only you could stop chewing over the issue, suddenly you *would* have that fateful trip to the supermarket where you get into a good-natured squabble with a shy veterinarian over the last loaf of sourdough.

It also assumes that those who have found their life partners are no longer burdened by useless, self-defeating thoughts. I can assure you that this is not the case.

But I did notice that the "why am I single" think-a-thons were particularly sticky. Especially since we're often encouraged to analyze this riddle—to write about it in our journals, or to answer workbook questions about the mistakes we made in past relationships and the emotional baggage we might be projecting into future ones.

Most of us don't doubt the value of pondering these questions in writing, but one recent study calls that idea into question.

In an experiment at the University of Arizona, psychologist David Sbarra and his colleagues tried to determine how a particular style of journal writing might help people experiencing emotional distress—in this case divorce. So they recruited ninety recently separated or divorced participants and divided them into three groups. The first was asked to explore their deepest feelings about their breakup in writing. The second was told to record the story of their divorce in a narrative structure that gave it a beginning, middle, and end. A control group kept a log of their daily activities, without any emotional content.

The results surprised the researchers: The control group fared the best. Especially for the subjects identified as "high ruminators," their best bet was *not* to create emotive prose about what it all meant but instead to keep a running log of such facts as what they had for breakfast and when they cleaned the rain gutters.

In hindsight, Sbarra said it makes sense that the broodiest among us would not be served by an exercise that asks us to mull a problem *even more.* "If a person goes over and over something in their head, and then you say, 'Write down your deepest darkest thoughts and go over it again,' we will intensify their distress," he said.

As a person prone to this sort of mental spinning, I find meditation useful because it's essentially an anti-rumination practice. But beginning students often protest the idea that letting go of their thoughts is a good idea. After all, thoughts can often lead to music, poetry, peace treaties.

It's true—sometimes we *do* have strokes of genius. But when I started taking an inventory, I quickly noticed that the vast majority of my mind's activity is either completely mundane ("What's for lunch?") or stuff I'd already thought before—many times. As Buddhist teacher Ethan Nichtern describes it, "I'm talking to myself, but I already know what I'm going to say."

In the movies, the hero has a sweeping epiphany—"I don't have to change! I'm perfectly lovable as I am!"—and that's the end. But in real life, backslides occur—again and again. So you have that grand moment of feeling your rock-solid inner worth and then . . . you lose it. The toxic thoughts come back. "Why am I still alone? Why did he leave me? Why do I have to go to another damn baby shower?"

It's like eating sour cream and onion potato chips (or insert your objectively disgusting but actually delicious snack of choice). You *know* they're terrible for you and that, from a culinary standpoint, they're an absolute zero, nothing but salt and fat and whatever scary chemical comprises the "sour cream." And yet, you think, "Oh, just one more."

The thoughts we keep on continuous loop are the result of what psychologist Mihaly Csikszentmihalyi calls psychic entropy. "The mind has a natural tendency to veer toward whatever is bothering us most," he told me in an interview many years ago. When we have an idle moment, we don't usually think, "Gee, I was lucky to grow up middle class in the wealthiest nation in the world," or, "Gosh, it's fortunate that I don't have a debilitating illness." Instead, we think, "I'm gaining weight," or, "My career is stalled."

There's an evolutionary reason for this—the wise cave-woman didn't spend a lot of time mulling her blessings; she needed to be on alert for sharp-toothed animals who might want to snack on her or her kids. We don't need this kind of vigilance when we're headed to a college friend's wedding weekend, but unfortunately that biological wiring is mostly unchanged.

The other reason we churn over this stuff is that it does provide some very tangible short-term relief. Pema Chödrön makes the analogy to scratching poison ivy. "It temporarily soothes the itch, but it also makes the poison spread," she said.

It helps to see those useless thoughts for the energy-sapping gremlins they are. They're the coworker who blabs at your desk while you're trying to concentrate; they're someone else's bad

AM radio at the beach. They have no meaning or content; they're just disruptions.

Meditation has helped me develop the skill of noticing—and thus disarming—those junk thoughts. The essential practice is both extremely simple and extraordinarily difficult. You sit on a cushion for minutes, hours, or even days and try to keep your mind completely in the present—to the breath coming in and out of your nose, to the triangle of light on the knotty wooden floor, to the smell of lunch (lasagna!) wafting from the kitchen.

And with this humble goal, you fail—repeatedly. But it's actually not failure. What happens is you realize you've spent the past five minutes debating about whether it's wrong to take the "vegetarians-only" option even if you aren't 100 percent vegetarian. How, really, they shouldn't be so strict because some of us are working very hard to cut out meat, even if we aren't perfect. At some point, you snap out of it—"oh, thinking." And then you very delicately set all of your brilliant arguments aside and put your focus back on the conch-shell sound of your breath. A few minutes later, you lose it again. "Why is that guy wearing a Hawaiian shirt in the meditation room? Doesn't he realize I'm going to spend the entire weekend staring at this hula girl? There should really be a rule about . . ." Oh, thinking.

The daily practice of calling myself on these micro-tirades means I'm quicker to catch myself when my mind gets hijacked by the stickier stuff, like reflecting back on the time a snotty acquaintance said, "You couldn't *pay* me to be single again." I can instead stop, take three breaths, and remember where I am— sitting at my desk on a rainy morning. I can see that no one is attacking or condemning me. Therefore, I don't have to fight anything. My old strategy: Staring into space and thinking, "Yeah, right, like anyone's clamoring to have *you* back in the dating pool. . . ."

Meditation helps me cut through the fog of those discursive thoughts and find that lovely clearing called sanity. When my mind flies off in a toddler-esque tantrum, it enables me to see it so that the wise and kindly mom inside me can say, "Hey, hey, what are you doing?"

Once again, this is not about self-improvement, or being single for that matter. It's about excavating that very wise, sane part of you that already exists.

We usually identify with the chip eater, the itch scratcher, but why not identify with your wiser side? The one who knows when to reach for the baby carrots, who knows that guy isn't so great. It won't stop the junk thoughts from coming, but with practice I've found it significantly loosens their grip.

20

YOU SHOULD HAVE MARRIED THAT GUY

On a not-so-cheery Christmas morning, Julia was cleaning the kitchen with her mother and sister when they told her they needed to talk. While Julia's nieces and nephews played in the next room, Mom and Sis explained that they were *worried* about Julia because she had broken up with Joe—who everyone agreed was the nicest of guys—and because she was thirty-eight. Perhaps she expected too much from relationships?

Furious and humiliated, Julia defended herself as she loaded the dishwasher. She had stayed with Joe for two years because she *wanted* it to work. She *wanted* to get married and have kids. She *wanted* to stop dating and stop being the spinster aunt at Christmastime.

She also wanted to feel desire for Joe, but she didn't. And after two years, she could no longer pretend it didn't matter. "He was such an incredibly nice person—so generous, so giving, and he wanted to get married. But it never felt right to me. I felt like I was forcing my feelings. I recall not being myself, not being fully honest. I knew I was dating such a wonderful person—a great uncle, great brother. So I was questioning myself. What's wrong with me? Why don't I want to marry this guy?"

Julia didn't know. She only knew that the ever-so-reasonable protestations of her family were pointless. She could not, would not settle.

He's a nice guy. We love him. He loves *you*. So what the hell is the problem?

The thirty-eight-year-old who breaks up with such a man will no longer be a puzzle to her loved ones, if she ever was—clearly she has sealed her fate with her arrogance and willfulness. *Hope you and your high standards stay warm tonight!*

But you don't necessarily have to have ended a relationship at such a geriatric age to wonder if your decision to "see other people" five or ten or twenty years ago has determined your destiny. A friend recently told me she thought she had bad karma for breaking up with the college boyfriend who adored her. "It's like I wasn't ready for it, for all that love," she said.

These remembrances of boyfriends past can be even more insidious than the more recent breakups—since in the latter case you at least have a fresh recall of all those silent dinners or petty snipe-a-thons.

But that guy from college or your early twenties? The one who picked you up at your house, and threw you birthday parties, and wondered aloud what your kids would look like?

He would have married you on the spot, would have hopped on a flight to Vegas without blinking. But you, foolish, foolish girl, were not ready to settle down. You cast him aside for some doe-eyed musician who was sensitive about everything except your feelings. Now your ex is happily married to some wiser woman and, according to Facebook, the two of them enjoy a life of middle-American splendor. You have seen their Disney Cruises, their kids' adorable first-day-of-school photos, the big pots of shrimp gumbo awaiting their New Year's Eve guests. It all could have been yours if you hadn't been so careless and vain.

For those of us who left good men for reasons that now seem vague—not being "ready," wanting "something more"—it's quite humbling to watch those calendar pages fly by without anyone reaching the ardor of that nineteen-year-old or even thirty-two-year-old beau. You thought there would be others who would love you just as much, and you were wrong.

And if you don't say it to yourself, or have concerned loved ones fretting over you, just wait—there's always another finger-wagging trend piece to remind choosy single women how dearly they are paying for their twenty-five-year-old arrogance. *Karma's a bitch!*

So let's talk about karma. First, the Buddhist notion of karma is not that you get rewarded and punished for all your good or evil deeds in one lifetime—karma plays the long game so you won't necessarily see the aftershocks of your saintly or selfish behavior by your eightieth birthday.

Second, if you, like me, are not convinced that reincarnation is real (I'm dubious of all afterlife theories, but please convince me otherwise!), then the whole concept gets pretty muddled. Sure, we all understand that being kind and helpful will likely make the world a friendlier place, and that there is generally quite a bit of blowback for being a jerk. But there's too much childhood hunger and wildlife-habitat destruction for any reasonable person to believe we all get what we deserve.

I took a course in karma as part of my Tibetan Buddhist studies program and honestly found it quite dull—high on lists and terms, low on assurances that the bitch at work who stole your idea will get hers. But the interesting part was that karma was not treated like a cosmic Santa Claus—separating the good little girls and boys from the bad ones. Instead, the basic teaching was this: We are all born with a particular disposition—likes, dislikes, talents, etc. We move toward certain things and away from others, and those preferences—and our response to them—determine our fate.

For example, say you choose a profession that is competitive and doesn't pay well. Say—oh, I don't know—freelance writer, just to pull out a completely arbitrary example. As a result of following your bliss, you find yourself at age thirty sleeping on a futon and squabbling with your roommates about who ate your muesli. Meanwhile, your techie classmate has a beach house and a new car every three years.

This is karma: Your choices have led you to very different outcomes. But you're not being punished for being "bad," nor has she been rewarded for being "good." You made those decisions based on your own unique abilities and preferences—it was just her good fortune that her desires and talents matched nicely with a well-paying career. Or, if she chose her profession for purely practical reasons—if she actually hates software programing—then it's her karma to spend forty hours a week doing something she doesn't like. Again, this doesn't make her a terrible person; just someone experiencing the consequences of a decision she made.

I'm not saying all choices are value neutral. If you're making a choice that's harming you or others—say, to snort cocaine every weekend—then deciding to do something different, like training for a marathon, will probably have a positive impact on your future. But there's no need to make it into a reward/punishment thing—it's just plain logic.

My friend thought she had "bad karma" because she wasn't ready to marry when she had the opportunity. But "not being ready" isn't being bad—it's not being ready. If she had made the decision to ignore her instincts and marry that guy, it's possible that after pushing through that apprehension she would have settled into a blissful union. On the other hand, she could have made both of them miserable by living a life she didn't want.

We can't know how things would have turned out in the alternate universe where we made different choices. We can only make the best decision we can with the information we have. Julia's decision might have looked ridiculous to her family, but in time a different story emerged.

A few months after breaking up with Joe, she heard from a man she had met (and quietly fallen for) a decade earlier at a wedding. "I had told a friend, I'd like to meet someone just like him," Julia said.

Back then, Matt was married; now he was divorced. They were engaged six months after their first date. "Meeting Matt confirmed for me that I wasn't crazy all those years. I knew what this would feel like and was holding out for it," said Julia.

So what exactly *is* settling? I spoke to two women whose stories seem helpful.

Throughout her twenties and early thirties, Laurie never had a serious boyfriend—the last one had been in high school. But she did have a very clear list of nonnegotiables for the man she wanted to marry. He would have to love the arts, not be religious, and want to live in Manhattan. Then she met a hilarious and charming man named Dave—who was a devout Christian who lived in the suburbs and couldn't care less about museums or the theater. They married when Laurie was thirty-five, and when we spoke they had just celebrated their tenth anniversary. I asked Laurie if she had settled, and she sounded incredulous at the very question. "Absolutely not! I feel lucky," she said from her home in Westchester.

Suzanne, the communications executive from Chapter 5, used to complain to her friends that she and her boyfriend weren't compatible because, for example, he was "into NASCAR." They told her she was nuts—who *cares* if he likes NASCAR! Suzanne stayed with him for two years.

When did she know it was time to break up? "When I couldn't stand to be in the same room as him. When I didn't want him to touch me," she said.

How do you know if you're settling? Easy. You're settling if you think you're settling.

Settling isn't mature—it's cruel. We all deserve to be loved and desired for who we are, for our essence—not our bank account, not our parenting skills, not because we happened to amble into someone's life at the biologically optimal time. When you settle for a man, you're preventing him from finding the woman who will love him for who he truly is. And *that's* bad karma.

21

YOU DON'T REALLY WANT A RELATIONSHIP

Also known as: "If you wanted a husband, you'd *have* a husband."

This comment comes from two places—the nice place and the not-so-nice one.

When you hear it from the nice place, it's usually a good friend or favorite aunt saying, *I see that you're an appealing person, capable of giving and receiving love. So if you're alone it must, on some level, be a choice.* It often has a go-sister vibe to it—*you're too cool to want a dumb old husband!* Sometimes they'll toss in a mild gripe about their own spouse—dirty socks on the floor, that sort of thing—and express wistfulness about how much fun it must be to have all that freedom, to go on dates, etc.

Your friend may or may not be correct in her analysis, but her intention is to say *I think your life is pretty cool, so own it. If you really wanted someone, you'd just marry some guy.* She will respect that you have a value system that favors love over lifestyle, and honesty over status.

However, you may have also heard a less generous view about why you, deep down, don't want to be in a committed partnership: You can't hack it.

Maybe you hear this directly, a remark by a snotty brother-in-law, who wonders aloud when you're going to "grow up" and "settle down" (as if you were roaming from flophouse to flophouse, earning cigarette money by playing cards). Or maybe you've just absorbed the cultural assumption that people stay single because they refuse to accept the rigors of marriage—that the only thing stopping you from joining the adults is your rigid insularity and inability to compromise. Why, you might have to negotiate differing toothpaste-tube-squeezing philosophies! What if he doesn't understand that there is only One True Way to arrange the remotes on the coffee table?

In the past, older singles were dismissed as batty eccentrics—the persnickety maiden aunt, the feckless bachelor uncle. That's harder to do now that singles are half of the population. Instead, single people have become part of a more ominous narrative—the "decline of marriage."

The age of first marriage continues to rise—it's now nearly

twenty-seven for women and twenty-nine for men. That might not sound so geriatric to you, but increased marital age along with a drop in the number of married couples has a lot of folks worried about those nutty commitment-phobes who are unraveling society's fabric. (The fact that many gay people are now heading to the altar apparently hasn't assuaged fears in this particular camp.)

In op-eds and big think-tank reports, the Official Worriers point out that non-college-educated women are becoming single mothers at a very high rate—a reasonable concern. Though the proposed solution is not to provide better access to birth control or a college degree (making them far less likely to have kids out of wedlock), but to pressure them to marry young. And that pressure isn't confined to high school dropouts—the "marry young" message extends to Ivy-League-educated women too.

Of course, they're doing this for your own good—*you'll be happier*! Oh, sure you won't get to do shots with your girlfriends till three a.m., and you'll have to give up that addiction to fifteen-hundred-dollar handbags. But trust us, it will be okay because once you marry, you will start to enjoy *deeper pleasures*. Once you say "I do," you'll go from boozy party girl to upstanding citizen—*just like that!*

The trouble with this fable is that, as I mentioned in Chapter 4, older brides do extremely well—especially if they have a college education. They have a lower risk of divorce, make more money, and are also more likely to have their children *after* they've married the father.

Indeed, far from undermining marriage, I would argue that picky, career-focused singles are one of its greatest allies. Because a funny thing happened while Americans were exercising their right to wait for the right relationship—the divorce rate dropped. The oft-cited 50 percent statistic is true for people who married in the 1970s, but with each succeeding generation the chance of splitting up declines. Economists Betsey Stevenson and Justin Wolfers examined the odds that married couples of various demographics would make it to their tenth anniversary. They found that college-educated women who married in the 1990s have a lower divorce rate (16 percent) than their cohorts who married in the 1980s (20 percent), who in turn had a lower rate than those marrying in the 1970s (23 percent).

With the caveat that correlations don't necessarily prove causality, Stevenson said the reason could be that people now are more likely to date more intensely before marriage. "They are thereby giving their relationships more kicks in the tires before trying out marriage. This may be one reason that the divorce rate has fallen. Some of the weaker relationships don't pass the test," she said in an email.

Marriage isn't in decline—it's stronger than it has been in

decades. And I contend that much of the credit should go to those of us who *didn't* cave to the social pressure to just get married already.

But don't expect to be thanked for all of that social-fabric mending. Singles continue to be society's solipsistic teenagers, while those who marry—especially those who marry young—are soberly upholding the values of a bygone era.

The funny thing is, as the scolds puff up marriage as the morally superior choice, they tend to use flag-waving words like "duty," "sacrifice," and "institution." The result is they make marriage sound less like a joyous union of two people and more like a deployment in Afghanistan.

I didn't marry my husband out of a sense of duty—I married him because he's awesome. I married him because he makes me laugh every day, because he has an intrinsic sense of compassion for the world's least powerful, and because he treats me the way I treat him—with love, kindness, and respect. Also, he's really cute. I'm not in an *institution*—I'm hanging out with my best friend.

That's how most of the late-in-life brides I know describe their marriages. Sure, some say marriage is "work" and many have noted the complexities involved in merging two very well-established lives into one—stepchildren, exes, etc. But the problem they *aren't* confronting is ambivalence—that colorless, odorless gas that corrodes so many relationships. This makes things much simpler when the invariable conflicts and compromises arise.

Indeed, economist Dana Rotz found that the older a couple's age at first marriage, the more time they spend together and the less frequent and more civil their arguments. (However, she notes that this data hasn't been parsed into specific age categories—we don't yet know if merely graduating from high school before marrying gets you this benefit.)

Consider Julia—my friend who was informed on Christmas morning that she expected too much from relationships. Julia had to give up quite a lot to be with Matt. She had to let go of her Brooklyn Heights apartment and move to a house in the Denver suburbs with Matt and his teenage son. She had to move hundreds of miles away from all her friends and family, to a city where she knew no one. In the span of a few months, she went from being a single woman who had her weekends free to write her novel to being a stepmother waking up at six a.m. to drive to hockey matches.

These things matter to Julia, but she doesn't feel sanctimonious about what's she's sacrificed because being with Matt is worth it—because she loves him. That's what happens when you hold out for the right thing. You don't feel superior—you just feel damn lucky.

Here's a thought: Maybe you've remained single well into adulthood because . . . you know what you're doing. Because there is something *right* with you. The culture may portray older singles as losers and narcissists, but the truth is the person who ends the mediocre relationship *before* marriage—or who never starts it in the first place—is a true pillar of the institution.

You didn't marry that very sweet guy who was constitutionally incapable of paying his electric bill. You also passed on the extremely well-respected attorney who somehow made you feel like shit. Perhaps what others call stubbornness or arrogance is actually good sense and intuition—and the maturity to know there are some things you cannot force.

22

YOU NEED PRACTICE

My original idea for this book was to tell the stories of other women who married after thirty-five. When my editor suggested I make the book about being single, my first thought was that I was no longer qualified. I had entered the Realm of the Married—I was one of *them*.

But then I realized women who marry after spending the bulk of their adult lives as single women are often the worst perpetrators of these stereotypes. You see this a lot in those "Happy at Last" profiles of famous actresses who married in their thirties or forties. Curled up barefoot on the couch, the celebrity confides to the reporter about how clueless she was during her single years—dating the wrong guys, being a people pleaser, etc.—but she fortunately wised up in time to collect the reward for all that (hard-won!) growth—the hunky husband making pasta carbonara in the kitchen.

Stories like this are meant to be inspirational—I did it, and so can you, sister! But the underlying message is that a happy romantic relationship isn't something you *find*, it's something you *earn*. You develop skills and accrue wisdom though the University of Other Relationships. This is where you hone your ability to negotiate cleaning schedules and fight fairly and assert yourself. It's where you finally learn to stop being attracted to men who are addicted to gambling or emotionally shut down. Post-breakup, you sift through the rubble of that pain and heartbreak for those gems of meaning and wisdom that will serve you in relationships to come.

This is a great thing—if you've had a lot of serious romantic relationships. But many of us haven't—or we've had them, but didn't find them so terribly educational. When I was single, this made me slightly anxious. Other people were getting their PhDs in relationships. I couldn't even pass the second grade!

Because I hadn't had many relationships, I worried I wasn't relationship material. Maybe I missed out on some fundamental life stage and now it was too late—years of solitude had molded me into a person who was incapable of sharing her life with another.

Mark and I had been dating for less than a year when he moved into my small one-bedroom apartment. I was forty years old and had never lived with a boyfriend. Naturally, I assumed I had a steep learning curve ahead. Instead, I was pleasantly shocked when I discovered it was . . . lovely. Yeah, yeah there were the usual adjustments about the equitable distribution of medicine-cabinet space and differing philosophies about reading magazines at the dinner table. We both have moods, and sometimes we fight. But bottom line: We like each other and we're grown-ups, so stuff generally works out.

Now, I realize the danger of holding up one's own marriage as a model of harmony: Just because we've lived peacefully together for seven years doesn't mean we aren't capable of screwing it up. Shit could happen—I know that.

But I also know I'm not the only relationship flunky who miraculously managed to skip fourteen grades. I've heard from many other people whose sparse Work History proved no impediment to the happy relationship they found at age thirty-eight or forty-two or fifty-seven.

"It has been effortless," said Ellen, a journalist who married for the first time at fifty-two. Despite a relationship résumé as spartan as mine, Ellen now lives happily with her husband and two cats in their tiny New York apartment. "The things that are a problem are not the marriage. It might be that he left something on the floor and the cats peed on it, but that's not a marriage issue. If you communicate well, negotiate, and get along, the other stuff isn't a problem," she said.

My friend Marcella—the artist in Chapter 2 who met her husband, George, after a nine-year dry spell—moved in with George about a year after they started dating. She too assumed she was in for some major growing pains and was instead surprised to find that she is very good at navigating the twists and turns of a long-term partnership.

"It feels funny to have gone from feeling like a colossal fuckup to realizing I'm actually really proud of how I conduct my marriage. Who would have thought I would ever feel like this after seeing myself as the bottom of the barrel for so long?" said Marcella.

If you're a smart, sensitive person, you're going to learn and grow—no matter what you do. If your serial-monogamist pal is gradually discovering how not to lose her identity in relationships, that's terrific. But perhaps the reason *you're* not taking that particular adult-extension course is—you don't need it. "You always see advice in dating books about how to stop dating the wrong guy," said Ellen. "But for me, that was like saying, 'For better health, stop smoking.' What if I don't smoke? I never needed advice on not dating the wrong guy—that's easy."

There are also many useful relationship skills that living on your own develops. You learn how to take care of yourself, and thus don't have to depend on your partner to buck you up after every failure or disappointment. You learn how to handle rejection, which means you can cope when your spouse comes home in a bad mood and shuts you out. You develop complete confidence in your ability to manage your life on your own, which means you have no problem ceding control over how the kitchen cupboards are organized or which retirement plan you choose.

I'll say it again—these kinds of skills are not prerequisites for a happy relationship, but they do come in handy. The wisdom I gained as a single woman did absolutely nothing to help me *find* a husband—that was pure, blind chance—but it did make life easier, then and now.

23

YOU'RE TOO OLD

When she was thirty-six, Sasha Cagen had what she describes as an utterly random impulse—to quit her job in Silicon Valley and travel throughout Brazil. With the proceeds from the sale of her social-network company, Sasha had the means to travel for many months, and her instincts told her that this would bring her out of the deep spiritual and sexual malaise she had been feeling for some time.

But she was afraid—not just because this was a huge life change, but because she was a single woman with a looming sense that she had an expiration date. "I thought, 'When I come back I'll be thirty-seven and no one will want to date me.

Everyone will screen me out of online dating and I'll be done,'" said Cagen, the author of *Quirkyalone: A Manifesto for Uncompromising Romantics.*

The deadline. That nagging feeling that you'll wake up on a fateful birthday and the gig will be up. You're no longer datable—send in the cats. Women get this message from many sources, but probably the most disheartening are the online profiles of men they're interested in meeting.

Is there anything that darkens a single woman's soul quicker than that line that begins "seeking women age . . ."? Or the really special feeling you get upon discovering that a man ten years your senior considers *you* too old for *him*?

It's useful information, at least. Who wants to be with a guy who isn't man enough to date his peers? But still, depressing.

Many men argue that this is nothing personal—it's not vanity or youth-obsession or fear of losing an argument that causes them to go young. They just want to have kids. If technology has enabled them to determine which online strangers they have a higher chance of having a family with, why not use it?

The worst part about this argument is . . . it's not completely irrational. The nice surprise of Internet dating is discovering that there is a live human being behind the screen name. But until you actually meet, we're all just pixels in the ether. If women could control for their date's ability to have kids with the click of a mouse, can we honestly say we wouldn't?

Of course, family-minded forty- and fiftysomething men should understand that if we're going to go all Darwin on each other, they're not exactly the strongest coyotes in the pack. Recent research indicates that men have biological clocks too, as scientists have found a correlation between advanced paternal age and conditions such as autism and schizophrenia.

That's the thing about biology—it doesn't care what's right, or fair, or appropriate for the way we live now. It just is. And that, unfortunately, has left many single people with a brutal choice: Hold out for the right relationship or have biological kids.

Shortly before I turned thirty-three, a well-publicized book came out informing women of their lousy chances of getting pregnant after thirty-five. This wasn't news to me—I had been awake that day in seventh-grade biology—still, it was no fun to read that fresh onslaught of opinion columns and magazine features informing me about my shriveling ovaries (but read them I did!). Since I knew ginning up female insecurity was a common media practice (and since seventh grade was a long time ago), I decided to fact-check with my doctor. At my next checkup, while sitting up on the papered table in a white smock, I told her to give it to me straight: "How much time do I have?"

She didn't miss a beat. "I wouldn't worry about it now, but if you get to be about thirty-seven or thirty-eight and you don't have a partner, you should talk to me about having a baby on your own," she said.

I must have looked a little shocked because she added, "That's what I would have done if I hadn't met my husband by then."

"I'm not going to do that," I said. "I don't want to be a single mother."

She nodded and told me about the baby she delivered to a forty-two-year-old the week before.

That made me feel slightly better, but the message was clear: If I waited for a husband to have a baby, I might not have one at all. That's exactly what came to pass.

Other late-marrying women I know had better luck—or just tried harder. One friend married at forty and subsequently had two children without any medical intervention. Others went down the long, hard IVF road and got pregnant (though others made the same efforts and did not).

My fortysomething friends and I made the best decisions we could at the time, and we got what we got. But for women now in their twenties and thirties, the options are changing in a very exciting way. A quiet medical revolution is taking place, as a small but growing number of women are freezing their eggs while single, and then carrying on with their lives.

The concept of egg freezing has been around for a while—my friends and I used to talk about it, but in the vague, non-committal way we might discuss emigrating to Canada or joining the Peace Corps. It was something to say when we were out of ideas.

Back when we were still carrying relatively young-ish eggs, the only viable way to freeze them was to turn them into an embryo. That was a problem, seeing as the whole not-knowing-the-father thing was the primary reason we didn't have kids in the first place.

Now, however, women can freeze their unfertilized eggs and expect to see the same success rate as fresh eggs if and when they undergo in vitro fertilization treatments.

Granted, the procedure is still very new, and quite expensive—between seven thousand to fifteen thousand dollars a cycle. And many single women are not charmed by the newest smug-married mantra, "You should freeze your eggs." Fair enough. But I do think we all need to take a moment and acknowledge how supremely wonderful this is—the most radical reproductive innovation since the pill. Women are now having babies with eggs they froze while single—with husbands they met years after putting their genetic material in cold storage. It's amazing and joyous and media reports should stop calling the women who take advantage of the technology "panic-stricken." Women aren't freezing their eggs because they're desperate or pathetic. They're doing it *because they can*.

As for us older gals, I admit I'm a bit envious of younger women for having this choice. But I'm still very grateful that my own doctor clearly explained my early-2000 options in such a nonjudgmental way—even if it freaked me out a bit. It made me clarify my priorities. If I had to choose between finding true love or having a biological child, I'd pick the relationship.

I've spoken to many women who faced down this tough decision too—women who made the same choice I did, women who decided to become single moms, and one woman who just went ahead and married that perfectly nice guy she met on Match (with whom she later had a child). As they tell their stories, I hear heartbreak and wistfulness sometimes, but I don't hear regret. The choice was tough, but it was *ours*.

As for Sasha Cagen, she was right that living in Brazil would revive her spirits, and wrong that she'd never date again. "It was completely untrue. People wanted me *more* than before and that continues to be true," she said from her current home in Buenos Aries, Argentina, where she's currently studying tango, running a couple of businesses (life-coaching and an online course called "Get Quirky") and writing a memoir about her experiences.

While she hasn't found a partner yet, Cagen says that the closer she gets to forty, the less she worries about it. That's the thing about hitting those big, bad birthdays—they happen and you realize that actually you have *not* suddenly morphed into a tragic Victorian spinster. You're still you.

"If I put aside the question of children, then it really doesn't matter what age I am," said Cagen. "I still have many years. I could take a pessimistic view, but why? There are so many reasons to be optimistic."

24

YOU DON'T KNOW LOVE

Or not *real* love anyway. Sure, you know plenty about silly infatuations and making out with guys in the backs of taxicabs, but not grown-up love.

Single people often feel compelled to report that they have had serious romantic relationships in the past. The person who lived with someone for five years or who was "almost engaged" gets more credit for understanding love than the person who has not. Being divorced wins you even more points. "It's viewed ironically that, 'Well, someone obviously wanted you enough to marry you and therefore you're not quite so bad,'" Pamela Paul, author of *The Starter Marriage*, told *USA Today* about the response she received after her own divorce.

Little credit is given to the person who has the sensitivity and intelligence to avoid the near-engagement or divorce—who takes months, rather than years, to realize the partnership isn't working. No due is given the person who refuses to be jerked around—thus compelling the jerks to move on to easier prey. It's assumed there is some love gene that you lack.

But here's what the perennially partnered don't understand: That love is always there, it just expresses itself in a completely different way.

One of Buddhism's primary teachings is to cultivate an awakened heart. Normally, we think of that in terms of having a romantic relationship—my heart is *on*, baby—versus being alone, where one's heart sleeps. But anyone who has lived a solitary adult life knows it's not like that.

You still have that energy, and while it does at times "sit in [your] belly like a stone" as Zoë Heller's narrator describes (see Chapter 7), it can also expand out—to the kind Indian grandfather at the corner market, to the restaurant worker taking his cigarette break on a back stoop, to the dazed morning faces on an early commute.

This is the sweet side of longing. Each encounter becomes magnified—the jokey banter with the guys at the butcher shop, the walk home with the woman you just met in yoga. Meeting a close friend for dinner isn't just a pleasant evening—it's life itself. Those two or three or seven hours of feverish conversation—of yelping in outrage at the sins of her small-minded boss, of gushing about the gorgeous novel you're reading, of deconstructing the latest male politician's take on women's reproductive organs—make all the other daily crap we endure more than worth it.

University of North Carolina psychologist Barbara Fredrickson says the connection we have during these warm encounters with friends and even strangers is love, a sensation that's biologically identical to the love we feel in its more celebrated forms—romantic, family.

Love, explains Fredrickson, isn't a cozy room you enter; it's not even a particular bond or relationship. Rather, it's the feeling of connection you have whenever eyes meet, smiles are returned, or jokes are shared. When "the boundaries between you and not-you—what lies beyond your skin—relax and become more permeable. While infused with love you see fewer distinctions between you and others," she wrote in *Love 2.0: How Our Supreme Emotion Affects Everything We Feel, Think, Do, and Become.*

Fredrickson and her colleagues discovered that the subjects of their study were able to bring more of these "micro-moments" of connection into their lives by practicing a form of meditation called loving-kindness.

The technique, which is taught at most meditation centers, is so simple it can seem like another insipid smiley-face cure. But although Fredrickson very much believes in cultivating positive emotions, she, like Oliver Burkeman, does not subscribe to the facile "be positive" school of thinking. Forcing your feelings doesn't work, creating instead what Fredrickson calls "toxic insincerity."

With loving-kindness meditation, you wish happiness to others through a short mantra—the one I use is "May you be happy. May you be at peace. May you be free from suffering." If genuine feelings follow, great. If not, that's fine too.

You start by wishing good things to someone you love in an uncomplicated way, like a child or a pet. Then you do it for yourself (many teachers will tell you to *start* with yourself; I find this order easier), then a friend, then a neutral person (an office-mate from another department, the woman who checks you in at the gym), and then a "difficult person." Finally, you gradually widen that circle to include everyone—in Boston, on the Eastern Seaboard, in the Western Hemisphere, on the planet, etc.

It sounds hokey, but when I practice this regularly I notice the edges around me start to soften—those warm micro-encounters *do* happen more often. When I see my "neutral person" on the street—the UPS guy, the teenage kid who lives around the corner—I feel that warm rush you get upon seeing an old friend. When I used to bump into my pain-in-the-butt upstairs neighbor—aka my "difficult person"—I might not exactly have felt *love*, but there was some compassion uprooting my hostility. The rote mantra "may you be free from suffering" helped me see that he was indeed in pain, hence the snippy, put-upon demeanor.

I know loving-kindness meditation makes me calmer and more compassionate. Fredrickson's research indicates that it can actually change people's body chemistry, as those who practiced it for slightly less than an hour a week were found to have significantly increased tone in the nerve that connects the brain to the heart. Called the vagus nerve, it's what coordinates a person's experience of love, supporting their ability to smile, make eye contact, and listen more attentively.

Fredrickson's research focuses on connections between people, but of course when you're unattached there are also many moments of solitude—where there isn't even a salesclerk to receive your warm regards. In those times I found myself falling in love with the way the light hit the trees in my neighborhood at dusk, or the sound of a distant train whistle.

Now that I'm with Mark, I still appreciate all this, but it's less intense. When you're in a couple, thoughts of friends, acquaintances, and strangers don't have as much space to brew. Moving through the world with a wellspring of love and affection for one (or, I guess if we had kids, three or four) is a cozy way to live, but it can also be a fairly closed loop of me-you-me-you.

In my meditation work, it often seems as if I'm trying to recapture a feeling that came more naturally when I was single—when that energy expanded out to the horizon and the returns were much more subtle than the rabbit-pellet rewards of coupledom.

I was struggling with this concept—the ineffable sense of connection you feel when you're alone, and that you pretty much lose when you join your life with another. The single people I mentioned this to nodded slowly as I grappled with it—they didn't have words to add, but they knew what I meant. My friend Bethany, who is married, noticed the difference on the other side of the equation, mentioning a single friend whom she looks forward to seeing more than any other. Evenings with Juliet, she explained, take on an almost romantic quality, because Juliet (her real name!) offers her such focused, unfettered attention. "I think everyone has a certain amount of reserves, and if you're giving most of that energy to the people you live with, there's not going to be as much for everyone else," said Bethany.

I realize that being alone doesn't necessarily make you a mystic. As I've exhibited to a mortifying degree, there's also lots of shutting down, of curling into a shell of me-me-me. And sure, couples are capable of popping out of their domestic bubbles. The difference is, when you're single there's no bubble to pop— or not one that's nearly as solid. It's just you and the vast open space.

Again, I'm not trying to set up a competition for who is more soulful—of course, intimate relationships offer their own opportunities for spiritual growth. But in a world that treats a forty-one-year-old single woman like a teenager who didn't get asked to prom, I think it's extremely important to recognize the unique wisdom of a solitary life—a wisdom that develops slowly over many years, that is fundamentally different from that of, say, the person who was between boyfriends for a year when she was twenty-six.

When you're experiencing that year-in, year-out challenge of being on your own, it's easy to ask the question "What does everyone else know that I don't?" I suggest you flip that around.

25

YOU SUCK

It's a story we've heard before: Mom writes sanctimonious blog about having kids, ignites the wrath of the Internet.

The infamous piece was an open letter to a (it turns out) fictional friend named Doris who embodied all the worst childless-single-woman stereotypes—clueless, self-absorbed, incapable of looking up from her phone: "If you're a mom, you know Doris. She's in her mid-thirties and thinks of herself as a career woman. She knows the clock is ticking. She says she's not panicking yet, but we know better—she's freaking out. . . . Sometimes Doris reminds me of my kindergartner—'What if I get sick tomorrow and can't go to school and I never learn to read?'

Sometimes Doris reminds me of my toddler twins—wanting whatever toy the other twin has."

Horrible, right? The whole piece was that bad—just breathlessly mean and condescending. And so the villagers took to their laptops, pounding the writer into mincemeat and branding her the "sanctimommy." (There were some extremely wise and thoughtful pieces mixed in with the nasty comments, but this made the overall effect even more damning.)

Then something unusual happened: The writer apologized. She actually read the criticisms, accepted responsibility for the vitriol she instigated and admitted (sort of) that her snarkiness was born of insecurity. "Some of the commenters are right. While I love that I've arranged a quirky work schedule so that I can drop everything when my kids need me, I totally resent the way I feel judged for putting my kids first. But that doesn't give me the right to attack anyone else."

It was an impressive display of honest self-reflection and humility. But it was also revealing for where it shopped short. That awkward, objectless grammar construction—"I totally resent the way I feel judged"—combined with the deflected blame (those awful people who think it's wrong to put your children first!).

I point this out not to pick on someone who has already been ground to a fine sand, but because it perfectly encapsulates the cesspool of bad feelings and judgment that comprises so much of modern women's discourse.

We feel hurt. We feel judged. And so we cope by throwing the poison darts back at someone else. *Yeah, being single is tough, but at least I'm not like Sally over there suffering through her miserable marriage.* She's *the one who should feel like a loser.*

The impulse to evangelize for your own life choices is apparently one most of us are afflicted with. In a series of studies, a team of researchers led by Stanford University psychology professor Kristin Laurin found that people who viewed their relationship status as unlikely to change—both married and single—idealized that status and favored those who shared it.

"When it comes to our relational status, we are rarely content to simply say 'being single works for me' or 'being in a relationship suits my disposition,'" the authors said in a paper called "The Way I Am Is the Way You Ought to Be," published in the journal *Psychological Science*. The researchers hypothesized that our need to rationalize our choices compels us to view our own status as the universal ideal—and thus look down on those who take a different route.

But as our hapless blogger discovered, foisting your insecurities on someone else doesn't diminish your pain—it only adds more pain to the world, and I think we can agree that there's quite enough of that.

So why then, if I'm advocating love and light, have I

structured this book around the infuriating and dismissive things people say to singles? Honestly, the initial idea sprang from my own welled-up bitterness. To paraphrase the sancti-mommy, I totally resented that I felt judged for trusting my instincts.

But more important, once I recognized the stupidity of this endless laundry list—I'm too self-conscious, I'm too stubborn, etc.—I was liberated from it. Once I convinced *myself* I was fine, I no longer needed to prove it to others—which in turn made me a nicer person.

The people in your life either understand where you're coming from or they don't. It's not your job to convince them that you're happy or a legitimate adult. It's also not your job to determine whether another's perceived self-satisfaction is born of genuine contentment or insecurity. Your job is to take care of yourself so you can meet others where they are.

There will always be another smug married coworker, another magazine cover story telling single women time is running out, another cultural critic hawking yet another calculated piece of flamebait.

It won't stop. But let us recall that much-quoted line from Eleanor Roosevelt: "No one can make you feel inferior without your consent." We know the phrase from coffee mugs and needle-pointed pillows, but how many of us truly heed it? It's so much easier to mentally lash out at the person who makes us feel like a bad mother or a shallow careerist than to face the "consent" part.

Again, you don't need to have high self-esteem or to "get right with yourself" to find a relationship—clearly, many happily coupled people are awash in self-doubt. But I do believe our society would be a far gentler place if we could all learn to face our insecurities and end the lifestyle arms race.

I once had an acting teacher tell me that if she accused me of being a psychopath, it wouldn't upset me. I'd be confident in the knowledge that I wasn't a heartless monster and the insult wouldn't stick. The accusations that sting are the ones we partly buy—or simply make up ourselves.

Too shallow.

Too immature.

Too unattractive.

Just fundamentally unlovable.

We get angry when others infer these things, but we all know who the harshest judge is. So here's another Buddhist saying I find useful: "When your demons come, offer them a piece of cake." Instead of trying to justify yourself or make someone else wrong in order to pump yourself up, try doing the completely counterintuitive thing: Let the demons in. Give those deep, dark feelings about yourself some breathing room.

Mind you, I don't mean tell yourself a big story about how much you suck—that will only compound those toxic thoughts.

Instead, take your intellect out of it and allow yourself to feel whatever you've been resisting. Treat those sensations like they're part of a scientific experiment. Note what happens in your body. Do you feel heavy, like your muscles are filled with sand? Is there a knot in the center of your chest? Is your stomach clenching? Just allow it to be there, just observe.

Normally, we treat difficult emotions like a judge or a boss—like a punishment for some wrong we've committed. When you no longer fear the feelings behind the judgments, then *you* become the boss. You can usher the disgruntled assistant into your office and allow her to rail for as long as she likes about why you're the worst. Her comments may hurt, and some may even be valid. But they don't swallow you whole. Because you're in the power position, you can hear her out without believing everything she says. You can step back and say, "It's true that I get anxious at parties and hate my thighs, but I don't think that makes me unlovable." Or "Yes, I do get a little nervous when a guy starts talking about having a family on the third date, but that's a pretty normal way to respond when someone you barely know projects so far into the future."

Kristin Neff, the self-compassion researcher (and a Buddhist, by the way), says that self-compassion is not just about buying yourself an ice cream cone—it's about accepting the fact that you're an ordinary person with flaws. That's why people with high self-compassion actually have an easier time seeing their failings—they're not invested in being better than anyone else. This makes them much more likely to take responsibility for their mistakes. *Wow, that was a really insensitive thing I just said. Sorry—I guess I was feeling a little jealous.*

The demons feed on resistance, so when you aren't afraid of them—when you can simply see them objectively and name them—they have nothing to work with. And when that happens, I've noticed that they very slowly leave.

26

YOU NEED TO FIGURE OUT "WHY"

One of the most profound changes I've noticed since I married is also quite subtle: I'm no longer compelled to answer for my relationship status.

No one ever asks "Why are you married?" even though the question is just as valid as "Why are you single?" After all, people marry for many reasons other than pure love—fear of being alone, a desire for biological children, economic security, social status, health insurance.

Mark and I married in our forties, are not religious (I study Buddhism, but I'm not a Buddhist), have no children, and lived together for four years before getting the state of New York involved. So the question "why?" is fairly valid in our case. But no one asks. Where there were once questions or gentle prompts about being career-focused, there is now honeyed silence.

In polite society, there's an understanding that inquiring about the reason two people marry is completely inappropriate. Singles are not afforded this privacy. Instead, the rude inquiries are wrapped in compliments about how attractive and together you are. *So what the heck's the deal?*

While sometimes the asker is merely making conversation, or just old—let's agree to give a free pass to anyone over seventy-five—it does appear that singles of a certain age make many people deeply uncomfortable and that these questions come from the same uncharitable reflex many have upon hearing of another person's cancer diagnosis. *Did she smoke?*

Even worse, of course, is when the asker is some cutie you meet at a party, especially when they sound like an employment counselor inquiring about a résumé gap—*what does everyone else know that I don't?*

And so the spunky heroine answers with a cheeky "Just lucky I guess!" Or maybe declares that she *is* picky—*got a problem with that?* The old chestnut "just haven't met the right guy" feels pretty neutral, but even this will likely prompt avuncular teasing about how surely one of the dapper groomsmen must have caught her eye.

The implication is that you need to explain yourself. That if you're not single by choice, you'd better be able to cough up a diagnosis for the concerned stranger. It's your job to assure them that you're either (a) workin' on it! or (b) entirely deserving of your situation. Suggesting that chance or circumstance is the culprit is unlikely to yield the desired effect—unless the desired effect is to be written off as a whiner or a victim.

The response that worked best for me was the one I gave that guy who asked what was wrong with me (and let's face it "Why are you single?" is a slightly more polite version of that question): "I don't know."

The starkness of the answer caught people off guard, I think, because I refused to do their dirty work—to give them an aberrant personality to match my aberrant situation. Instead, I directed the discomfort back to its proper recipient—the person asking the intrusive question.

I didn't realize it at the time, but I was claiming the married person's privilege—the right to have your life choices be no one's business but your own.

Why are you single? Maybe there are many reasons, maybe there are no reasons. The real question is, why are near strangers so often compelled to demand answers?

27

YOU'LL SPEND THE REST
OF YOUR LIFE ALONE!

Melanie Notkin was standing on the shoreline with a close friend, a married mother of three, when her pal said the thing she knew many others had been thinking: She should have a baby on her own.

Notkin had always wanted children, but she also wanted to fall in love and marry the father of those kids. Unfortunately, that hadn't happened yet. Notkin explained that she didn't want to be a single mother, not only because it would be incredibly hard and stressful, but because she feared it would leave her too time-strapped and exhausted to date. She'd hold out for love.

"I just don't want to see you alone for the rest of your life," said her friend.

"But this *is* the rest of my life," said Notkin. "Right here and right now. This is my life."

While it isn't exactly what she had planned, it's a great life. Notkin owns and runs Savvy Auntie, and has a thriving writing career, a vibrant social life, and of course, heaven-sent nieces and nephews. She's still hoping to meet that special person, but she no longer views her life as a waiting period for that day.

Youth is a time of striving, of preparing for "the future." It's when you study hard, fetch coffee for cranky bosses, and make out with guys in dark bars. It's when you make mistakes, fumble, and gradually figure out who you are—or at least cobble together what you'll later call "your personality."

Marriage has traditionally been the time we declare youth over. Now you have arrived. Welcome to the rest of your life.

So what happens when that day comes decades later than expected, or not at all? When does "the rest of your life" start?

Posters of sunrises and dewy meadows inform us that *today* is that day, but sometimes it sure doesn't feel that way. Today feels a little too much like yesterday, and the day before that. Yes, you're no longer delivering coffee—maybe you even have someone fetching *yours*. Your apartment is probably nicer. Maybe you don't shop at H&M anymore and you probably went ahead and bought yourself a good set of china.

But these things likely happened gradually. As opposed to the whole wedding whirligig, where relatives, parties, expensive appliances, new addresses, and high thread-count sheets all descend at roughly the same time. Marriage gives you a distinct sense of Before and After, and of course children mark time like nobody's business, always morphing and mushrooming into larger and more complicated shapes and sizes.

One of the most challenging things about being a single childless adult is that time seems more fluid and undelineated— months, years, and even decades can bleed into one another. There is less a sense of a road with distinct mileage markers—it's more a wide-open field. In this untethered state, it's easy to feel as if you might float away if you don't at least get some two-hundred-dollar frying pans in the cupboard.

But as I listened to Notkin talk about her life, I realized how much she sounded like my Buddhist teachers. She explained that she enjoys dating much more now that she's in her forties, because she no longer brings a heavy sense of Is He the One? to every coffee meet up. She has learned to roll with whatever-the-hell each date is, to be in it without a lot of conditions about how things are supposed to go.

"When you're older and dating, the bumps and bruises of it—you almost celebrate them. It's kind of like getting a zit. Oh, he upset me. He got a reaction out of me—wow!" she said.

As one of my meditation teachers might say, this is pretty deep practice. This is singlehood's great gift: It puts you squarely in the present and grounds you in the reality that life is much less solid than we usually believe.

Marriage can create an illusion of permanence. This is our life, and it's not going to change. See us plot our twenty-year plan. It can camouflage the unsettling truth: Nothing is permanent, nothing is assured. The ground is always shifting beneath our feet.

After my *New York Times* piece ran, one commenter complained about the late-in-essay reveal that I was now married. "I thought she was one of us," she said.

"I *am* one of you," I said to the computer. But I also knew what she meant. On our wedding night, I had a minor—but not unpleasant—identity crisis. "Who *am* I now that I'm married?" I said to Mark. "I'm *the single girl*. That's who I *am*."

We cling to our marital and parental statuses as if they are immutable parts of our character. The Single Girl! A Mom! Child-Free and Loving It!

But these identities are shape-shifting all the time. Singles marry, marriages end (or alter beyond recognition), and Mom—the woman who was once the epicenter of your most searing needs and desires—becomes a nice old lady you call on Sundays and take to lunch. (A nice old lady you love very much—hi, Mom—but who over time starts to depend on *you*, rather than the other way around.)

We're always in flux—even the cells of our body regenerate every seven years. We are, quite literally, completely different people than we were a decade ago.

From this perspective, the question "How can I live my life fully as a single person but also be open to a long-term partnership?" is absurd. Enjoying things as they are but also working toward change isn't living a second-class life; it's living a full life—one where you clearly see what Tibetan Buddhists call "the truth of impermanence."

Many people in Notkin's life—in particular those who hit their culturally and biologically appointed deadlines—don't quite get this. "Those who love us and want good things for us are sometimes not satisfied with our lives not wrapping up in a bow," she said.

But one of the best things about turning forty, she says, is that her life has become so unfathomable to her loved ones that the commentaries have stopped. "This is the gift of forty," she said. "In a good way, they start to give up on you. I'm free of the questions."

YOU ARE HERE

I met Dan shortly before my twentieth high school reunion. I'd
found his nice-looking picture and modest profile online, and
by our third date my feelings had slowly evolved from "huh,
maybe" to "wow, I think I really like this guy."

It was a presidential election year, and Dan had recently
raised eighteen hundred dollars for the Democratic Party by
holding a fund-raising yard sale with friends. I liked this about
him—his roll-up-your-shirtsleeves approach to political and
environmental activism, and the plainspoken way he described
it. "The problem with the environmental movement is that it's
always 'save the planet,' which is so abstract. The planet will
survive. What we really need to say is 'save the people,'" he said.

A sweet, smart guy who cared about the larger world—the more we talked, the cuter he got. We kissed on his Brooklyn stoop, and I spent the cab ride home indulging the idea that things were finally, finally snapping into place.

This warm glow carried me through the reunion, where I was one of five unmarried people. The conversations were what you'd expect—my classmates told me about their family vacations and their kids' after-school activities, and I told them about my writer's life in the city. I felt self-conscious about being single, but managed to hold steady as people swapped children's pictures and discussed their town's after-prom provisions (Proms! Their kids were already going to proms!). This was, as my teachers said, *the practice*—not sitting on a cushion, but facing resistance wherever it arose. Anyway, soon I would return to my real life, the one where being thirty-eight and single was not so unusual. Soon I'd be back in Brooklyn, where there was a sweet liberal boy who wanted to kiss me.

When I got home I sent Dan an email saying I was looking forward to telling him about the reunion. A day later, I received a very kind reply explaining that he had started dating another woman at about the same time we met, and over the weekend "things took off."

That same week, my dog Taffy died.

I cried for days. I cried over Taffy and over Dan, but mostly for the state of my life. I was thirty-eight. I had gone to my hometown and told the story of how my life had turned out. That was that.

I can't remember how many nights I woke up at four a.m. crying, or how many times I spent dinners with friends staring blankly into space, fiercely unwilling to be consoled. I was alone. I would always be alone. And it didn't matter how many books I read or how many downward dogs I did or how much I nurtured my friendships or how kind I was to strangers. Nothing mattered.

And of course, I thought about her—the Chosen One. Dan probably met her at an antiwar march or a phone bank or a MoveOn house party. (Oh, Josh M. and Cara B., why did I spurn your kind invitations!) Maybe he signed her Greenpeace petition. Maybe she showed up, coin purse and price stickers at the ready, to pitch in at the yard sale.

Thus, a new reason to hate myself. How right he was to pick this girl, this *better* girl. After all, what had *I* done to make the world a better place? A few assorted volunteer projects, but on balance, not much.

I spent a couple of weeks in this cloud of grief and shame. Despite my training otherwise, I turned my disappointment into a larger thesis about why I'd always be alone. I might be someone you'd want to date, or sleep with, or have beers with, but not someone you'd ever love, because love was for other women, better women, women who had some ineffable goodness that my gray soul lacked.

I was in the midst of this thought stream one drizzly Sunday afternoon, imagining Dan and the Chosen One planting yard signs and poring over voter data. Finally, wiser me kicked in: *If you feel bad about not being politically active, then be politically active.*

After all, the reason I had made up—like, completely fabricated out of nothing—for Dan's rejection was significantly different from my past speculations. In those cases, there wasn't much I could do about not being pretty enough or smart enough or cool enough. But "not dedicated to community service enough"? The barrier to entry was as high as a croquet wicket.

And if my conscience had been unsettled—well, good. After all, I *talked* about politics all the time, specifically my growing fear that the country's civic life was slowly unraveling. So why *wasn't* I spending more time in the public square?

That's when I decided to do something both embarrassing and wonderful: Copy him. I organized a building-wide Democratic Party fund-raising stoop sale. Clearly my motives weren't pure. Obviously, I was still under the sway of my crush, making this irrational attempt to win him back—even though I knew full well it wouldn't work.

But I barely thought of Dan on that sunny September Saturday, as my friend Jessica and I sold old clothes and paperback books from our co-op's front yard. Business was hopping all day as neighbors stopped to chat and cheerfully overpay for the cause. After making the donation online—six hundred dollars—I took myself out for coffee.

The cafe had a little waterfall, which I stared into while sipping my latte, the whooshing sound melding with clinking forks and light jazz. I had a funny feeling, one I couldn't quite identify. I watched the backlit water rush over the faux stones for ten minutes or so until it finally hit me: *Oh, this is what it's like to feel good about yourself.*

After all those years of tunneling through the mud, I finally hit that little wink of gold, my basic goodness. After all the protests—"I'm *not* too picky!" "I'm *not* afraid of commitment!"—I found that place where none of the lists or reasons mattered: *I am as good as anyone else.*

Whether I found a partner or not, basic goodness was there—*had always* been there. It wasn't there because I was attractive or talented or special. It wasn't there because I had *grown.* It was there because I was a human being, that's it.

The world doesn't tell us we have basic goodness. Instead it says, *You're almost there, sweetheart. There's just these one or two or eighteen thousand things we need to tweak.* Your better self is right around the corner—look at her in that convertible, honeyed highlights billowing. See her rocking that PowerPoint presentation. Or whipping up a salad in her modern kitchen (granite and stainless steel!), and who is that mystery man coming up behind her with a kiss on the temple and a strand of perfect pearls? Go ahead—press your nose up against the glass, get a good long look at the woman you could be if you could *just pull it together.*

And yet, we never get there. Perfect you is always several steps ahead, briefcase swinging.

The stoop sale didn't transform my self-image: That had been quietly going on for years, in a process that was as slow and tedious as climbing that godforsaken StepMill at the gym. Notice thoughts; breathe in pain. Notice thoughts; breathe in pain. Notice thoughts; breathe in pain.

Not that you necessarily have to be so deliberate about it. I think the very act of *being* single provides enough hard-core strength training to put anyone's psyche into fighting shape.

You get over that guy, and then you get over the next one. You write to five people online and hear from zero. You tell that very nice management consultant, "I don't think this is a match."

You go alone to your niece's wedding, where you sit up straight and say nice things about pictures of people's kids. Three years later, you go to her baby shower and your cousin asks if there is "anyone special in your life" and while you contemplate saying "actually there are *lots* of special people in my life—like you!" you know that's not what she means so you smile and say, "Not at the moment."

You have a shitty day at work and briefly wish there was

someone to rub your feet and listen to you rant. There isn't, so you draw yourself a bath.

You push through the resistance, maintain your poise through the indignities. And one day find you have a strength you never knew existed.

When that happens, very often no one notices—maybe not even you. Some slight or heartbreak occurs. You're at a dinner party and a man old enough to be your grandfather makes a move. A married woman ten years your junior frets openly about her biological clock. The cutie sitting next to you looks horrified when you recall a too-long-ago Olympic moment. *Wait—you were* born *then?*

It's the kind of thing that once crushed you, but tonight it just . . . doesn't. You take another bite of crab cake and the whole thing disperses and floats away with the dust motes. You turn to the woman next to you and ask how the real estate sales are going.

Nothing has happened, but everything has happened.

So there you are, in that beautiful clearing: the meadow where the tall grass billows; the shoreline where mist rises over the churning river, the mountaintop where bluebirds and sparrows swirl overhead; the rooftop where the city buzzes below.

You're enjoying your life, feeling "good with yourself." But you're still waiting for that shoe-drop moment. *Hi, is this seat taken?*

I never found a way to make that feeling go away, to douse

that slow burn in my chest. Instead, I learned to simply let it be there, a passing shadow that came and went.

So What Then?

I was once in a meditation class where the instructor asked everyone to close our eyes and imagine we were on our death-beds. "Think of all the moments of your life that you're grateful for," he said.

Sounds corny, but after you've spent the past half hour listening to your breathing, this sort of thing can be revealing. Because you don't necessarily think of the big-ticket events, like graduations or trips to Paris. Instead, you remember searching for old bottle caps in your backyard when you were eight, or sitting in the supermarket parking lot with your teenage pals, drinking watery beer and eating barbecued potato chips. The moments you're grateful for aren't always even particularly "good" times—there's the chilly spring evening you took a deep breath, walked into a coffee shop, and said, "Excuse me, are you Rob?"

When I skimmed through my single years—that is, *most* of my years—I thought about the time I bumped into some friends at a street fair and we all decided to get a table at an outdoor bar and listen to the band. I thought about a dinner party I had for five female friends where everyone stayed until two a.m., bitching about their jobs and their ex-boyfriends and refilling each other's wineglasses. I thought about the New Year's Day I walked the length of Manhattan listening to Spiritualized.

Happiness was there the whole time. The problem was, I was so specific about the *type* of happiness I wanted that I far too often ruined a good thing. I wanted the sort of happiness that made me feel normal. I wanted romantic love, yes, but I also wanted the security and social status that surrounds it.

As someone who now has that, I confess it's no small thing. Being with Mark means dumping file cabinets full of worries into the incinerator. I love my life with Mark, but I see now that my life was just as rich when I was single—it was *always* vast and gorgeous.

I would bitch about how difficult it was to travel on my own—no one to stand with the suitcases while I bought a magazine. True, true. But there is also spending that hour sitting at that cute little espresso stand, watching the jets fade into the sky. I'd feel shitty about weekends and holidays when I had no plans, but that unfettered time also meant spending two whole days writing an experimental short story or reading *Tess of the d'Urbervilles*. I'd complain that it was taking forever to find this *one* person, but the unwavering search meant I was meeting many *other* people.

It meant driving across the state of Wyoming with Suki and

Jonathan, the three of us slack-jawed as we watched the landscape change from mountains to tundra to English pastoral every thirty miles.

It meant making roast chicken for my book club on my thirty-seventh birthday, Daphne and Kristin hustling around the kitchen with me as the other members arrived a little too soon.

It meant standing on a Virginia train overpass with Coleman and Janet at midnight, the bridge vibrating and the wind suctioning upward as the freight roared by.

It meant swapping apartments with Scout and living in Seattle for a month, just to see what it was like.

It meant discovering that the good people of Cleveland are surprisingly friendly when you march up to their doorstop, clipboard cradled in your arm, and remind them to vote on Tuesday.

There were many edgy, uncomfortable emotions that compelled me to do this stuff—a desire to meet men, a need to prove to myself that I was hitting my fabulous-single-girl marks.

But although the experiences were often born of discomfort, they were also some of the best times of my life. When I was single, I crisscrossed the country, trying to find my real life. How could I not see that I was already there?

RESOURCES AND
RECOMMENDED READING

Brené Brown, PhD, LMSW. *Daring Greatly: How the Courage to Be Vulnerable Transforms the Way We Live, Love, Parent and Lead* (Gotham, 2012).

Oliver Burkeman. *The Antidote: Happiness for People Who Can't Stand Positive Thinking* (Faber and Faber, 2012).

John T. Cacioppo and William Patrick. *Loneliness: Human Nature and the Need for Social Connection* (Norton, 2008).

Sasha Cagen. *Quirkyalone: A Manifesto for Uncompromising Romantics* (HarperOne, 2006).

Pema Chödrön. *No Time to Lose: A Timely Guide to the Way of the Bodhisattva* (Shambhala, 2007) and *The Wisdom of No Escape* (Shambhala, 1991).

Gail Collins. *When Everything Changed: The Amazing Journey of Women from 1960 to the Present* (Little, Brown, 2009).

Stephanie Coontz. *Marriage, a History: How Love Conquered Marriage* (Penguin, 2006) and *A Strange Stirring: The Feminine Mystique and American Women at the Dawn of the 1960s* (Basic, 2010).

Mihaly Csikszentmihalyi. *Flow: The Psychology of Optimal Experience* (Harper Perennial Modern Classics, 2008).

Bella DePaulo, PhD. *Singlism: What It Is, Why It Matters, and How to Stop It* (DoubleDoor, 2011) and *Singled Out: How Singles Are Stereotyped, Stigmatized, and Ignored, and Still Live Happily Ever After* (St. Martin's Griffin, 2006).

Barbara L. Fredrickson, PhD. *Love 2.0: How Our Supreme Emotion Affects Everything We Feel, Think, Do and Become* (Hudson Street Press, 2013).

John M. Gottman, PhD, and Nan Silver. *The Seven Principles for Making Marriage Work* (Three Rivers Press, 2000).

Zoë Heller. *Notes on a Scandal: What Was She Thinking?* (Henry Holt, 2003).

Betsy Israel. *Bachelor Girl: The Secret History of Single Women in the Twentieth Century* (William Morrow, 2002).

Eric Klinenberg. *Going Solo: The Extraordinary Rise and Surprising Appeal of Living Alone* (Penguin, 2012).

Amir Levine, MD, and Rachel S. F. Heller, MA. *Attached: The New Science of Adult Attachment* (Tarcher Penguin, 2010).

Rachel Machachek. *The Science of Single* (Riverhead, 2011).

Samhita Mukhopadhyay. *Outdated: Why Dating Is Ruining Your Love Life* (Seal, 2011).

Kristin Neff, PhD. *Self-Compassion: Stop Beating Yourself Up and Leave Insecurity Behind* (William Morrow, 2011).

Melanie Notkin. *Savvy Auntie: The Ultimate Guide for Cool Aunts, Great-Aunts, Godmothers, and All Women Who Love Kids* (William Morrow, 2011). (And check out her forthcoming book, *Otherhood*!)

Tara Parker-Pope. *For Better: How the Surprising Science of Happy Couples Can Help Your Marriage Succeed* (Plume, 2011).

Susan Piver. *The Wisdom of a Broken Heart* (Free Press, 2010).

Sara Elizabeth Richards. *Motherhood, Rescheduled: The New Frontier of Egg Freezing and the Women Who Tried It* (Simon & Schuster, 2013).

Mari Ruti, PhD. *The Case for Falling in Love? Why We Can't Master the Madness of Love—and Why That's the Best Part* (Sourcebooks Casablanca, 2011).

Chögyam Trungpa. *The Sanity We Are Born With: A Buddhist Approach to Psychology* (Shambhala, 2005); *Training the Mind and Cultivating Loving-Kindness* (Shambhala Classics, 1993); and *Shambhala: The Sacred Path of the Warrior* (Shambhala Classics, 1984).

Christine B. Whelan, PhD. *Why Smart Men Marry Smart Women* (Simon & Schuster, 2006) and *Marry Smart: The Intelligent Woman's Guide to True Love* (Simon & Schuster, 2009).

Articles and Studies Cited

American Society for Reproductive Medicine. "Fertility Experts Issue New Report on Egg Freezing. ASRM Lifts Experimental Label from Technique," Oct. 22, 2012.

Lisa Arnold and Christina Campbell. "The High Price of Being Single in America," TheAtlantic.com, Jan. 14, 2013.

Olivia Barker. "Singled Out by Society's Stare," *USA Today*, Feb. 13, 2005.

Oliver Burkeman. "The Power of Negative Thinking," *New York Times*, Aug. 4, 2012.

Bureau of Labor Statistics. "Spotlight on Statistics: Women at Work," Mar. 2011.

Ewen Callaway. "Fathers Bequeath More Mutations as They Age," *Nature*, Aug. 22, 2012.

John T. Cacioppo, Stephanie Cacioppo, Gian C. Gonzaga, Elizabeth L. Ogburn, and Tyler J. VanderWeele. "Marital Satisfaction and Break-ups Differ Across On-line and Off-line Meeting Venues," *Proceedings of the National Academy of Sciences*, June 2013.

Elizabeth Cohen. "Freezing Your Eggs: The Costs and Other Realities," CNN, Oct. 6, 2011.

Paula England and Jonathan Bearak. "Women's Education and Their Likelihood of Marriage: A Historic Reversal," Fact Sheet for Council on Contemporary Families, April 11, 2012.

Naomi Gerstel and Natalia Sarkisian. "Marriage: The Good, the Bad, and the Greedy," *Contexts*, Fall 2006 and "Single and Unmarried Americans as Family and Community Members" fact sheet for Council on Contemporary Families, Sept. 15, 2011.

Eric Klinenberg. "Solo Nation: American Consumers Stay Single," *Fortune*, Jan. 25, 2012.

Kristin Laurin, David Kille, and Richard Eilbach. "The Way I Am Is the Way You Ought to Be," *Psychological Science*, June 26, 2013.

Leslie Mann. "Women Say 'I Do' to Education, Then Marriage," *Chicago Tribune*, May 2, 2012.

Melanie Notkin. "Why I Choose Love Over Motherhood," *Huffington Post*, Aug. 21, 2012.

Pew Research Social & Demographic Trends. "Barely Half of U.S. Adults Are Married—A Record Low," Dec. 14, 2011.

Michael J. Rosenfeld and Thomas J. Reuben. "Searching for a Mate:

The Rise of Internet as a Social Intermediary," *American Sociological Review*, 2012.

Dana Rotz. "Why Have Divorce Rates Fallen? The Role of Women's Age at Marriage," Dec. 20, 2011. Paper under review.

David Sbarra, Adriel Boals, Ashley Mason, Grace Larson, and Matthias Mehl. "Expressive Writing Can Impede Emotional Recovery Following Marital Separation," *Clinical Psychological Science*, Feb. 15, 2013.

Sue Shellenbarger. "Single and Stepping Off the Fast Track," *Wall Street Journal*, May 23, 2012.

Betsey Stevenson and Justin Wolfers. "Divorced from Reality," *New York Times*, Sept. 29, 2007.

Buddhism Starter Kit

There are many great places to learn to meditate or study Buddhist principles—from your local yoga studio to Zen center. I practice a Tibetan Buddhist lineage called Shambhala, which has centers in most major cities (Shambhala.org). The Insight Meditation Center, founded by Sharon Salzberg, is also very popular (dharma.org).

Most meditation centers host public talks that are inexpensive or free, so that's a good way to find a fit. If you live in a place where yoga and meditation centers are not plentiful—or existent—check out Susan Piver's Open Heart Project: susanpiver.com/open-heart -project. Susan is an amazing teacher who offers online meditation classes. There are also retreat centers where you can study for a week or weekend—I'm partial to Sky Lake Lodge in Rosendale, New York.

Before I ever walked into a meditation or Buddhist center, I was reading books on the subject. Here are some of my favorite Buddhist writers:

Pema Chödrön. Smart, funny, compassionate, and wise. I give her books to friends when they're going through a rough time and return to them myself when life has got me down. I started with *The Wisdom of No Escape* (Shambhala, 1991) and *When Things Fall Apart* (Shambhala, 2002), but really they are all great.

Tara Brach, PhD. *Radical Acceptance: Embracing Your Life with the Heart of the Buddha* (Bantam Books, 2004).

Mark Epstein, MD. *Going to Pieces Without Falling Apart* (Broadway, 1999).

Steve Hagen. *Buddhism Plain and Simple* (Broadway, 1998).

Sakyong Mipham. *Turning the Mind Into an Ally* (Riverhead, 2003) and *Ruling Your World* (Doubleday, 2005).

Sharon Salzberg. *Lovingkindness* (Shambhala, 2002).

ACKNOWLEDGMENTS

It was my great good fortune to be edited by the wise and insightful Meg Leder. Meg helped me shape this book from the very start, and her comments and suggestions throughout the process made this a much better book. I'm also grateful that several other people on the Perigee team took the time to meet with me and review my work. Special thanks to John Duff, Marian Lizzi, Jeanette Shaw, Lisa Amoroso, and Lindsay Boggs.

My agent, Gail Hochman, was the first champion of this book—she's a wonderful agent and a good egg. So is Jody Klein.

Huge thanks to my readers: Meghan Daum, Caitlin Dixon, Mary O'Connell, Kris Puopolo, and Michele Suchomel-Casey. And to Bethany Lyttle, Paul Braverman, Marialisa Calta, Daphne

ACKNOWLEDGMENTS

Eviatar, Michelle Goodman, Paula Kamen, David Kidd, Suki Kim, Helene Stapinski, and Nancy Woodruff for advice on titles, structure, and other publishing-related matters.

I spoke and corresponded with many people as I wrote this book, but since some did not wish to be named I'd like to simply thank all the people who took the time to speak with me or answer my questions via email. You made this book . . . this book.

Parts of this book were originally published as essays in the *New York Times* and *Self*. I'm grateful to Daniel Jones, Christina Tudino, and Paula Derrow for helping me shape those pieces.

I've been fortunate to have many wonderful Buddhist teachers, who have informed this book in countless ways, including but not limited to: Vegan Aharonian, John Ankele, Jenny Bates, Frank Jude Boccio, Stephen Clark, Steve Clorfeine, Andrea Darby, Ciprian Iancu, Ethan Nichtern, Susan Piver, and Laura Simms. Two other important teachers: Acting instructor Elizabeth Browning and my first writing teacher, Verlyn Klinkenborg.

Thanks to my family. To my parents, Bob and Mary Alice Eckel, and my brother, Mark Eckel, for always supporting me. And of course, deep thanks to my dear husband, Mark Holcomb, who was worth the wait.